Walter Doe

**Important religious truths**

Walter Doe

**Important religious truths**

ISBN/EAN: 9783337263706

Printed in Europe, USA, Canada, Australia, Japan

Cover: Foto ©Lupo / pixelio.de

More available books at **www.hansebooks.com**

# IMPORTANT
# RELIGIOUS TRUTHS.

COMPILED BY

REV. WALTER P. DOE.

---

PROVIDENCE, R. I.
A. CRAWFORD GREENE & SON, BOOK AND JOB PRINTERS.
1883.

# PREFACE.

### THE OBJECT STATED.

The author and compiler of the following miscellaneous truths, publishes them because they seem to him to be of transcendent importance. They seem to him to discuss earnestly, practically and briefly, the most momentous subjects which can occupy the attention of the human mind. And in the numerous extracts and quotations, he has endeavored to select the best thoughts of the best authors, and condense their expression into the briefest form.

Therefore he earnestly solicits their careful perusal from those into whose hands they may providentially fall.

And if these truths shall in like manner commend themselves to their impartial and honest judgment, as of very great value and benefit, demanding their immediate reduction to practice, so that they shall profit by them in their personal experience, he invites them to assist, by their wide and free circulation, in the promotion of the principles advocated in them, so as to advance the religious reformation of Society, and prepare men for heaven, and thus glorify their Creator.

"For Godliness is profitable unto all things, having promise of the life that now is, and of that which is to come."

WALTER P. DOE.

Providence, R. I., Jan. 1. 1883.

# CONTENTS.

PREFACE—The Object Stated..................................iii

## (1) THE TRUTH OF THE BIBLE PROVED.

### CHAPTER I.
Harmony of Nature and Revelation........................... 1

### CHAPTER II.
Harmony Between the Doctrines of the Bible and Divine Providence.............................................. 11

### CHAPTER III.
The Divine Inspiration of the Bible........................ 16

### CHAPTER IV.
The Character of Christ of Supernatural Origin............. 21

### CHAPTER V.
The World Without Christ................................... 25

### CHAPTER VI.
The Good Effects of Christianity the Best Evidence of Its Divine Origin........................................ 30

### CHAPTER VII.
The False Philosophy and Demoralizing Influence of Infidelity Prove that it Must be Untrue................. 39

## CHAPTER VIII.
Experimental Evidence of the Truth of Christianity...... 43
## CHAPTER IX.
The Consistent Christian Life the Best for Time and the Safest for Eternity................................ 56
## CHAPTER X.
Responsibility for Belief............................ 60
## CHAPTER XI.
Sincerity Insufficient. ............................. 66

## (2) GOD AND HIS MORAL GOVERNMENT.
### CHAPTER XII.
A Supreme Moral Governor Indispensable.............. 78
### CHAPTER XIII.
The Perfect Goodness and Severity of God in Government. 82
### CHAPTER XIV.
Erroneous Views of God Corrected..................... 86
### CHAPTER XV.
Mystery of Mysteries. Sin and Suffering............... 90
### CHAPTER XVI.
Why do the Best of Christians Sometimes Suffer in this Life, More than the Worst of Sinners............. 93

## (3) RETRIBUTION.
### CHAPTER XVII.
Probation Limited to the Present Life................. 97
### CHAPTER XVIII.
No Second Probation During the Intermediate State, or During the Sleep of the Bodies of the Dead........ 101
### CHAPTER XIX.
Christ and Eternal Punishment....................... 107
### CHAPTER XX.
Unreasonableness of Universal Restoration by Chastisement and Disciplinary Education.................. 117
### CHAPTER XXI.
The Consistency of Eternal Punishment with God's Benevolence and Goodness....................... 123

## (4) TRUE RELIGION.

**CHAPTER XXII.**
The Nature of True Religion Benevolent, and Voluntary Obedience to God, Not Merely the Excitement of Right Feelings. .................................. 126

**CHAPTER XXIII.**
The Service of the Lord in Secular Duties .............. 132

**CHAPTER XXIV.**
Who are the Righteous? .................................. 136

**CHAPTER XXV.**
Difference Between Morality and Religion............... 142

**CHAPTER XXVI.**
The Mere Moralist Guilty and Condemned............... 145

**CHAPTER XXVII.**
Humility and Self Estimation............................ 148

**CHAPTER XXVIII.**
Full Assurance and Witness of the Spirit............... 152

**CHAPTER XXIX.**
Way of Eminent Holiness................................ 154

**CHAPTER XXX.**
The Highest Practical Piety............................. 157

**CHAPTER XXXI.**
The Christian's Secret of a Happy Life................. 226

**CONCLUSION.**
Sermon—Divine Message. Text: "I have a message from God unto thee. Prepare to meet thy God. Be ready. The time is short.".................... 238

# (I.) THE TRUTH OF THE BIBLE PROVED.

## CHAPTER I.

### HARMONY OF NATURE AND REVELATION.

There is harmony in the teachings of Nature and divine revelation. Hence it appears that ignorance and depravity are the chief causes of infidelity.

Although revelation is necessarily added to the light of nature that men may learn to worship their Maker and the duty of benevolence towards men, the truthfulness of christianity is entitled to and demands our belief, chiefly on account of its holy and reformatory influence, in proportion as men embrace and practice its perfect laws and holy precepts. The Scriptures must have been written by good men or bad men, or by God himself. But good men could not have been guilty of false pretences in writing it; bad men would be unwilling and incapable of writing such a holy book, which condemns all sin and their souls to hell forever. Therefore, the Holy Scriptures must have been written by holy men under divine inspiration for the religious instruction of the human family. And all who will follow Christ's perfect example and obey his perfect precepts may test the truth of christianity in their own experience, that it makes them holier and happier here, and fits them for the blessedness of heaven hereafter.

Hence said Jesus, "If any man will do his will he shall know of the doctrine, whether it be of God."

Although the supreme object of divine revelation is the teaching of religious and spiritual truth for the guidance of mankind in their relations to God and each other, its incidental allusions to physical phenomena and the laws of Divine Providence, must ever be found in harmony with each other so far as finite human reason can comprehend and interpret correctly, the vast and infinite subjects to which they relate.

But as our investigations into the works and word of the infinite Jehovah from the nature of the case must ever be limited, we must always expect that in science and religion alike there must be "some things hard to be understood."

In both nature and revelation there are taught important facts which are plain and easily understood, but in each are unfathomable mysteries.

Both being the product of the same infinite mind, they alike bear the divine impress. If there are profound and insoluble mysteries in the works of the Creator, it is reasonable to expect them in His holy word. Therefore to deny the obvious and plain truths of either because there is mystery or seeming inconsistency connected with them is very unreasonable. For by honest and diligent study we may learn enough of nature to be of great practical utility and enough of revelation to secure our eternal salvation.

Dr. McIlvaine takes broadly and boldly the ground that "the Holy Scriptures were given to reveal moral and spiritual truth, and it is no part of their object to teach the truths of science, upon which, consequently, they are no authority.

He further says:

"These allusions in the Scriptures to physical phenomena, in order that they should be absolutely correct and unchangeable, must have been made in forms of expression corresponding, not to the present, but to the still future and last developments of science; in which case they would have been unintelligible to us, and to how many of the coming generations of mankind we cannot tell. . . .

"The Scriptures always speak of natural phenomna in forms of expression originally derived from the impressions which they make upon the senses, but often modified by philosophical conceptions in explanations of them, such as prevailed at the time among the people to whom the revelation was communicated. For certainly it was no part of their object to correct these impressions or conceptions, however erroneous they might be. . . .

"By the adoption and consistent application of this principle of interpretation, the malignant enemies of true religion—that seed of the serpent who are permitted to bruise the heel of the seed of the woman whilst he crushes their heads—would be deprived of their deadliest fangs."

"When we speak of Nature," says Dr. Parr, "we mean all the works, visible and invisible, in the universe of God. These works have from very remote ages, been the subject, more or less, of human investigation. As advances were made, and new discoveries disclosed what were supposed to be new facts, were formulated and set down as scientific truths to stand as accepted science until some subsequent investigator comes along, upsets them and proves positively that something else was the accepted truth of science. Thus investigation has gone on, deepening and widening and increasing with the years, until at the present, scientific research has reached a point of thoroughness and correctness never before attained.

"Investigators properly rank as theistic and atheistic. The former pursue their course into Nature's mysteries 'as seeing Him who is invisible,' seeking truth for its own sake, and recognizing God as the author of all truth, scientific as well as revealed.

"The latter class of investigators have a theory to establish, and to this end and this alone they work. That theory excludes God from the universe."

Hume, the historian, gives a comfortless view of the sober, honest thoughts of a godless philosopher. He says: "I am affrighted and confounded with that forlorn solitude in which I am placed by my philosophy. When I look abroad, I forsee on every side dispute, contradiction, and distraction, I find nothing but doubt and ignorance. Where am I or what? From what cause do I derive my existence, and to what condition shall I return? I am confounded with these questions, and begin to fancy myself in the most deplorable condition imaginable, environed with the deepest darkness."

Such are some of the legitimate results of the brightest intellectual attainments in philosophy and science when unaccompanied by the light of revelation.

Considering the definition of Nature given in the outset of this article practically correct, we ask what are the laws of Nature about which we hear so much said, and through and by which the great works of the universe are accomplished? In the sense of qualities inherent *in* matter, laws or properties impressed *on* matter, there is no such thing. It is simply the will and voice of God crystalized or materialized with reference to physical things. Their harmonious operation is but the will of God tangibly expressed, one form of revelation. A correct knowledge of natural or physical truth is not as easily obtained nor as readily understood as of revealed truth, but God is the Author of both.

It is properly conceived that an all-wise Author should not contradict himself. Revelation says— "In the beginning God created the Heaven and the Earth." And that "God formed man of the dust of the ground and breathed into his nostrils the breath of life and he became a living soul." Some say they have obtained more rational and reliable explanation than this, from the book of Nature. They tell us that matter is eternal, and that some time in the very far distant past, by some kind of fortuitous coming together of particles the Sun, Moon, Stars and Earth with all their satellites and with all their beautiful arrangements for day and night and the seasons were effected and organized; that man has his origin at the bottom of the ocean in a little moneron, and had to travel for ages through myriad species of animals, clean and unclean, to reach his present state. We can't help feeling a desire to say, how do you know all this? But it has been demonstrated that the mingling of sea-water with alcohol gave a feculent precipitate, which when separated from the liquid proved to be the identical meneron of Haeckel and protoplasm of Huxley—the Adam and Eve of all life, according to advanced modern science. It is but a precipitated sulphate which any chemist can produce at will in his laboratory. This experiment was shown to Prof. Huxley and which forever blasted that scientific delusion. It is claimed by atheists that geology and paleontology contradict the Scriptural account of creation. But the Bible was never given to teach geology, paleontology, astronomy nor any other branch of philosophy or physical science, and so it is not authority on these subjects. It was intended to reveal moral and spiritual truths. Suppose in those early days before there was any physical science properly so-called, and when the world believed in the geocentric system of the physical universe, the Bible had assumed to be scientific authority on all subjects to which it made allusion, and had spoken in strictly modern scientific terms, it is manifest that it would have been wholly unintelligible to the former generations of man. And perhaps not much less so to us, as science is continually changing its nomenclature and terms of expression, and God only knows when it will arrive at any definite standard or the exact truth. To say the sun rises and sets was a proper and well-understood expression in the days of Joshua, as well as now; and if he had commanded the earth to stand still instead of the sun, he would have been thought a lunatic and treated worse than Galileo was.

Scientific terms and theories will, perhaps, always be more or less in a state of mutation. Before the days of Galileo the earth was thought to be immovable and the heavenly bodies to revolve around it. Before Dr. Priestly's discovery, in 1774, oxygen and gaseous bodies were considered only modes of common air. The arteries in the human body were thought to contain air until Harvey made the discovery that they carried the oxygenated blood. Light, heat, electricity and even life have been considered only modes of motion, but now are proven, thank God, in the "Problem of Human Life" to be substantial entities.

The wave-theory of sound, centuries old, taught throughout the scientific world, as a settled and unalterable scientific truth is now numbered among the exploded scientific humbugs of the past. Evolution as taught by Darwin, Haeckel, Huxley and others, and thought by its friends to be impregnable, has also been utterly demolished and its champions are now afraid to open their mouths or make a scratch with their pens in its defense.

These exploded scientific theories are like the devils that entered the swine—their name is legion. Lyell says that in 1806 the French institute named not less than eighty geological theories that were hostile to the Scriptures, but not one of them are held now. The president of the British Scientific Association, and the vice-president of the American Academy of Natural Science, have admitted that the "whole foundation of theoretic geology must be reconstructed." When scientists agree among themselves it will be time to proclaim a conflict between Nature and Revelation, and to ask us to lay down our Bibles that have guided millions to the heavenly world and accept their ever changing theories instead. We are not afraid of scientific *truth*. Let it come. It only adds more light and proves the unity of the Divine Saviour and the Great God of Nature.

When men know the real truths of science and their relation to each other, there will appear no conflict, but the harmonious blending of evidence of the existence and efficient presence of the one Eternal God. Philosophers will then say with David "the heavens declare the glory of God and the firmament showeth His handiwork." Scientists will join Paul in saying, "the invisible things of Him from the creation of the world are clearly seen, being understood by the things that are made, even His eternal power and Godhead." And all men will say truly, it was a fool that "said in his heart there is no God."

And we can reasonably believe the doctrinal teachings of the Bible on all religious subjects, as infallibly inspired, and as entirely trustworthy as a religious guide. As of supreme authority, perfectly trustworthy, as inspired of God. Therefore, after learning its perfect authority and truthfulness, we are rationally and imperatively bound to believe all its divine teachings as of ultimate and supreme authority in matters of doctrine, though it teach things beyond our finite reason.

An eminent and aged disbeliever wrote thus to a young inquirer:—

SIR: I am very busy, and am an old man in delicate health, and have not time to answer your questions fully, even assuming that they are capable of being answered at all. Science and Christ have nothing to do with each other, except in as far as the habit of scientific investigation makes a man cautious about accepting any proofs. As far as I am concerned, I do not believe that any revelation has ever been made. With regard to a future life, every one must draw his own conclusions from vague and contradictory probabilities. Wishing you well, I remain your obedient servant, CHARLES DARWIN.

*Down, June* 5, 1879.

One desires that some one else could have cotemporaneously written the young man, as Paul wrote to a young man once, in those infinitely wiser words:

"O, Timothy! guard that which is committed unto thee, turning away from the profane babblings and oppositions of the knowledge which is falsely so called; which some professing have erred concerning the faith."

Paul was an old man, yet when the day of his departure was at hand he declared his joyful expectancy of a future life of eternal blessedness.

He wrote to his beloved Timothy, his son in the gospel, thus:

I charge *thee* therefore before God and the Lord Jesus Christ, who shall judge the quick and the dead at his appearing and His kingdom;

Preach the word; be instant in season, out of season; reprove, rebuke, exhort with all long-suffering and doctrine.

For the time will come when they will not endure sound doctrine; but after their own lusts shall they heap to themselves teachers having itching ears;

And they shall turn away *their* ears from the truth, and shall be turned unto fables.

But watch thou in all things, endure afflictions, do the work of an evangelist, make full proof of thy ministry.

For I am now ready to be offered, and the time of my departure is at hand.

I have fought a good fight, I have finished *my* course, I have kept the faith:

Henceforth there is laid up for me a crown of righteousness, which the Lord, the righteous judge, shall give me at that day: and not to me only, but unto all them also that love his appearing.

# CHAPTER II.

## HARMONY BETWEEN THE DOCTRINES OF THE BIBLE AND DIVINE PROVIDENCE.

(ABSTRACT.)

When the doctrines of the Bible are faithfully compared with the established order of Divine Providence, they are found to harmonize with each other.

" The heavens declare the glory of God, and the firmament showeth His handiwork."

The law of the Lord is perfect, converting the soul; the testimony of the Lord is sure, making wise the simple. The Scriptures declare that the God of Divine Providence is also the God of Divine Inspiration. The God of Divine Providence and the God of Grace and Redemption is the same Divine Being. All that we see of Him in His providence is in harmony with what we see of Him in His word. His providence and His word never contradict each other or misrepresent their Almighty Author. Therefore all the objections urged against God's sovereign grace in the christian scheme, lie against the actual order of events and must consequently be invalid and futile.

It seems to us that the light of Nature is a revelation of existing facts in the universe and the whole system of doctrines in the Bible is a revelation of the actually existing facts of christianity. The doctrines for example, of the trinity of the Godhead, the divine government, human depravity, Christ's atonement, spiritual regeneration, future happiness and misery are simply statements of what has been, of what is, and what will be in the divine administration.

In illustration of this truth let us examine the analogy between the teachings of Nature and revelation, concerning the fact of *human apostacy*.

The Scriptures teach us that the single transgression of Adam was the beginning of that long train of sin and wretchedness, which has passed upon the inhabitants of our world.

Now we acknowledge that it is mysterious to us, how a perfectly holy being, as Adam was, should yield to temptation. But as the result of the fall, observation confirms the teaching of revelation that "the heart of the sons of men is full of evil, and madness is in their hearts while they live." And this Scriptural doctrine concerning the consequences of Adam's first sin upon all his posterity is in harmony with the law of divine providence.

Witness the effect of the drunkard's conduct upon his relatives and descendants. As has been inquired, who is stranger to the common fact that his intemperance wastes the property which was necessary to save a wife and children from beggary, that his appetite may be the cause of his family being despised, illiterate and ruined, that the vices which follow in the train of his intemperance often encompass his offspring, and that they too are profane, unprincipled, idle and intemperate?

Again. Let us notice the harmony between revelation and divine providence in reference to the atonement of Jesus Christ.

And here let it be observed that the Christian scheme is not responsible for the fall of man. It finds him deeply involved in sin, entirely destitute of holiness; and proposes a remedy for an existing state of evil. It proposes by the doctrine of substitution, by the sufferings and death of Jesus Christ, to restore the penitent sinner to the favor of God.

Now let us inquire, is it not according to the analogy of Nature that calamities which are hastening to fall on us are often put back by the intervention of another? In illustration of this, let us recur to the helpless and dangerous periods of our early life.

"Did God come forth directly," asks a writer, "and protect us in the period of infancy?" Who watched over the sleep of the cradle and guarded us in sickness and helplessness? It was the tenderness of a mother, bending over our slumbering childhood, forgoing sleep, and rest, and ease, and hailing toil and care that we might be defended. Why, then, is it strange that when God thus ushers us into existence, through the pain and toil of another, that he should convey the blessings of a higher life of blessedness by the groans and pangs of a higher Mediator? Now we affirm that in every instance of the substituted sufferings or self-denial of a parent, there is sufficient of analogy to the sufferings of Christ for us to show that it is in strict accordance with the just government of God, to remove all objections to the peculiarity of the atonement.

But it may be said that it seems unreasonable that the heathen should suffer both here and hereafter through ignorance of this atonement without a knowledge of which, according to the Bible, none can be saved.

The heathen obviously are not guilty, as all men are in christian lands who do not seek salvation through Christ's atonement, but they lie under the curse of the fall and their own personal sinfulness, from which Christ came to deliver all penitent believers. Of course they will suffer only in proportion to their sins and the light which they reject. "Where little is given little will be required."

The Hindoo suffers and dies under the rage of a burning fever. The fault is not that he is ignorant of the virtues of quinine, nor is he punished for this ignorance of its healing qualities, but he is lying under the operation of the previous state of things, from which medicine contemplates his rescue.

"For there is no respect of persons with God.

For as many as have sinned without law shall also perish without law; and as many as have sinned in the law shall be judged by the law;

For not the hearers of the law *are* just before God but the doers of the law shall be justified.

For when the gentiles, which have not the law, do by nature the things contained in the law, these, having not the law, are a law unto themselves;

Which show the work of the law written in their

hearts, their conscience also bearing witness, and *their* thoughts the mean while accusing or else excusing one another;"

Still further. Let us contemplate the analogy, the harmony, between the demands of the Holy Scriptures and Divine Providence, in reference to the doctrine of regeneration.

The Bible teaches that without a change of heart and life none can be saved. And we all know that men often experience a sudden and most important change and revolution of feeling and purpose in temporal matters.

Who is ignorant, inquires the writer above quoted, that from infancy to old age the mind passes through many revolutions,—that as we leave the confines of one condition of our being, and advance to another, a change, an entire change, becomes indispensable, or the whole possibility of benefiting ourselves by the new condition is lost. He who does not change the idle and playful habits of childhood into habits of industry as he enters the period of manhood, will commonly find his hopes of accumulation blasted forever.

We ask then why some revolution similar in results (we mean not in nature) should not take place in reference to the passage from time to eternity in order to render his condition blessed in heaven?

But the Scriptures teach that the spiritual change is both the work of God and the work of man. Like all other mercies this great blessing hangs on the will of God. "Without me ye can do nothing." But we also know that by a free, voluntary trust in the Almighty grace of our Saviour we shall be successful in working out our " salvation with fear and trembling."

# CHAPTER III.

## THE DIVINE INSPIRATION OF THE BIBLE.

### (a.) A DIVINE REVELATION NEEDED.

The light of nature discloses to mankind the existence of their Creator. By studying His works and dispensations they may learn, not only His self existence, but many of His natural attributes, such as eternity, immutability, omnipotence, independence, omnipresence, omniscience, unity, goodness and wisdom.

And in contemplating these fundamental truths, they may learn that He sustains to them the relation not only of Creator, but of Preserver, Proprietor, Lawgiver, Governor, Final Judge and Disposer. Having these facts before them, they may learn by the appropriate use of their mental and moral faculties that he justly claims their confidence, their love, their worship and their service.

But while the light of nature is comparatively obscure and indefinite on these points, it is silent on many other truths, which are essential for men to know, in order to the attainment of the highest holiness and happiness.

We imperatively need a supernatural revelation, to teach us that God possesses the attributes of holiness, justice, truth and mercy. We must have an inspired volume to teach the moral perfections of the Lord and the plan of redemption through Christ, as well as the kind of worship and service which He requires, and the destiny of the righteous and the wicked beyond the present life.

Without a revelation of the Divine will we cannot understand why our present existence should be so short and uncertain, or why our journey through life should be so often beset by trials and afflictions. Without the Bible we are incapable of gaining any plausible solution for the Divine permission of sin or suffering; neither can we understand why his justice and benevolence should sometimes doom the righteous to greater trials than the wicked in this life. It is reasonable, therefore, to expect, in view of God's natural perfections, and our own necessitious condition, that He should grant us a written revelation. Thus we are prepared to appreciate with favor—the solemn declaration concerning the Holy Bible.

"All Scripture is given by inspiration of God." Holy men of God spake as if they were moved by the Holy Ghost. Therefore, the Bible must be plenary inspired as an infallible, trustworthy guide in religion.

(*b.*) INSPIRATION DEFINED.

The plenary inspiration of the Bible is an extraordinary Divine agency, operating through or upon teachers while giving instruction whether oral or written by which they were taught, what and how they should write or speak. In other words, in writing the Sacred Scriptures the penmen were perfectly under Divine guidance, on all strictly religious subjects, and wrote as they were moved by the Holy Ghost. There was a supernatural guidance or assistance of the Holy Spirit afforded to the sacred writers, guarding them against error and leading them to write just what God saw to be suited to accomplish the ends of revelation.

(c.) PROOF OF DIVINE INSPIRATION.

The sacred writers themselves claimed to be under the influence of Divine inspiration when they were employed in writing the Holy Scriptures. Those who wrote the Old Testament declare that they saw visions; that the word of the Lord came to them; and that they were divinely authorized to sanction their warnings, their reproofs, and their predictions with a "thus saith the Lord."

"By all these modes of expression," says Dr. Emmons, "they solemnly profess to have written, not according to their own will, but as they were directed and moved by the Divine Spirit. And this testimony of the prophets to their own inspiration is fully confirmed by the united testimony of the apostles."

(d.) VALUE OF THE BIBLE.

If the Bible is an inspired book, it is of priceless value. Nothing can be more important than an acquaintance with the mind of God. Hence, this volume must be infinitely more precious than all other books combined. No wonder then that the devout Psalmist should exclaim: "O how love I thy law; it is my meditation all the day. How sweet are thy words unto my taste; yea, sweeter than honey to my mouth. I love thy commandments above gold; yea, above fine gold. The law of thy mouth is better unto me than thousands of gold and silver." And in the nineteenth Psalm he gives his reasons for this high appreciation of the word of God. "The law of the Lord is perfect, converting the soul; the testimony of the Lord is sure, making wise the simple. The statutes of the Lord are right, rejoicing the heart; the commandment of the Lord is pure, enlightening the eyes. . . . The judgments of the Lord are true and righteous altogether. More to be desired are they than gold; yea, than much fine gold; sweeter also than honey and the honeycomb."

Again, if the Bible was written by Divine inspiration, it is an infallible rule of faith and practice. Whenever we have any uncertainty about the correctness of our doctrinal sentiments or religious duties we can here learn what is true and right. The law and the testimony must ever be our supreme counselor and perfect guide. We can never be justifiable in appealing from Scripture to reason, but we must always appeal from reason to the inspired word of God. Again, if the Bible was written by inspiration, we see why it has produced such a wonderful influence in the world. All books which have been published have had but little influence in convincing pursuading and governing men, in comparison with this volume of inspired truth. When attended by the spirit it has converted millions from sin to holiness.

Again, if "all Scripture is given by inspiration of God," it is reasonable that its sacred pages should bear the impress of Divinity. All human productions are marked with imperfections; but a book composed by the Almighty should bear the marks of divine perfection and divine wisdom. If the face of Nature reflects the image of its Creator, it is reasonable that His inspired word should bear the superscription of its Divine Author.

Thus we perceive that His holiness and wisdom are disclosed in the prohibitions and penalties of this sacred revelation. This book gives us the most important instruction, which we could never learn elsewhere. Has it not, therefore, every internal mark of its Divine origin and authority? And shall we not embrace it as our guide in life and support in death?

Finally. If the Scriptures were written by Divine inspiration, all are bound to search them, that they may know their present moral character and their prospective condition in the future world. The Bible plainly teaches that all men are either righteous or wicked, saints or sinners, that there is a radical distinction between him that serveth God and him that serveth Him not. In this book exceeding great and precious promises are made to all, who are striving to please the Lord by an obedient and holy life.

And, Oh, what deadful threatenings are denounced against impenitent sinners, to be inflicted in the interminable future. "These shall go away into eternal punishment: but the righteous into life eternal."

# CHAPTER IV.

## THE CHARACTER OF CHRIST OF SUPERNATURAL ORIGIN.

### (EXTRACT.)

What think you of the Christ? is an interrogation the most fundamental and all-engrossing that has ever been propounded to men. For more than eighteen centuries, it has been the most vital question among all classes. Even unbelievers cannot let it alone, for they feel that their eternal well-being might depend upon a proper answer to it.

We do not understand by Supernatural, something contrary to all means; but that which is superhuman, and above the common laws of Nature. We believe that the Supernatural comes within the domain of law, but it is a higher law than any with which we are now acquainted. All Nature at first originated in the miraculous, and it is impossible for the world to get rid of the idea of miracle. In all this, however, we believe there was profound method. The mission of Christ into this world was not without means; but it was the grandest methodical arrangement of which man can form a conception.

The Jews did not originate the character of Christ, for it was the opposite of all their preconceived ideas of the Messiah. It arose far above any conception of which the Jewish mind was capable. It could not have taken its origin among the gentiles, for it was entirely too Jewish for them. That it did not originate with the disciples of Christ is shown in the fact that even after His resurrection from among the dead, it required miraculous power to make them fully comprehend the completeness of His character. We must, therefore, conclude that the character of Christ was of *Supernatural origin*, and that it required the Great Artist to present to the world such an original and such a perfect picture.

The teaching of Jesus proves His divine origin. It can not be said of Him that He simply taught good things; for every thing he taught was absolutely perfect. At the conclusion of His grand sermon on the mount, the people were astonished at His teachings; for He taught with authority, and not as their scribes. The first seven beatitudes of that sermon should convince every honest mind of the divine mission of Jesus.

They refer to traits of character and to states of mind, and are paridoxical; for the world's conception of the man who is superlatively blessed has always been the opposite of what is taught in them. The doctrine was new and strange not only to the heathen world, but also to the most cultivated students of the Jewish faith. The truth of all these maxims has been fully realized by all that have accepted and practiced them. They make up a perfect character.

The life of Jesus corresponded to His teachings; for He perfectly practiced what he taught. Not a man, among the keen-eyed critics, or the vilest opposers of Christianity, has been able to produce a single instance where Jesus violated in practice what He had taught. In this Jesus stands alone; for He is the only teacher who has a perfect practice, and the only one who has perfectly practiced what he taught. How account for this without admitting the divine authority of Jesus Christ?

The teaching and the life of Christ have stood the test of time. What has become of the philosophers who were contemporary with Jesus? With the exception of a very few they have gone into forgetfulness, to be heard of no more until the unfolding of the records of the last judgment. What has become of the great statesmen of Greece and Rome? With the exception of a few, they too have passed from the records of time, and have gone into the shades of forgetfulness. What has become of the Jewish doctors who lived in the days of Jesus? Their names have also perished, and they have left but few foot-prints on the sands of time. The name of Jesus acquires more influence day by day. How understand this without accepting the divinity of His mission?

The admissions of those not favorable to Jesus in His day are sufficient to show that His teaching was of superhuman origin, His question to the Jews about the baptism of John silenced them, and showed that they despised the truth. They admitted that he cast out demons, and tried to explain it away. Judas, the traitor, understood all the private counsels of

Jesus, and he went to the chief priests to confess that he had betrayed the innocent. The wife of Pilate and even the governor himself, pronounced Jesus innocent. After the resurrection of Christ, the guard came into the city to report the fact, and was hired by the Jewish priests to tell an absolutely unreasonable falsehood.

# CHAPTER V.

## THE WORLD WITHOUT CHRIST.

In support of this truth I quote the following extract of a sermon.

Matt., iv, 16: "The people which sat in darkness saw a great light; and to them which sat in the region and shadow of death, light did spring up."

If during our lives it had always been daylight we might not realize how much we are indebted to the sun for light. This glow and brightness which reveals everything, which shows colors, which shows us the path, is diffused in the atmosphere. Present when the sun is obscured, in-doors as well as out. We avail ourselves of it without thinking of the sun, and in a thousand nooks and corners when the sun is not visible. We would not know but that it belonged to the atmosphere, an inherent part of it, if we had not experienced the darkness of night, when the sun is beneath the horizon, and then witness the change its rising makes. So with principles of ordinary morality and benevolence. In this nineteenth century and in this land of ours, these principles somewhat diffused, known, admired, become respectable, many even worldly motives for practicing them, so that very many practice them to a limited extent who are not disciples of Christ. Such men are apt to forget that they are at all indebted to Christ for this moral enlightenment and wide diffusion of noble sentiments and influences. Priding themselves on their morality and benevolence they are apt to say, "This is religion enough; we try to be honest and kind; we are under no obligation to Christ, and have no need of a Saviour." It is a good thing for such to go back and see what the world was without Christ, even as regards ordinary integrity and kindness. Contrast the opinions, sentiments and practices prevailing when Christ came, with the precepts He gave, and the ideal He presented of character, and you will see how well the text expresses it. "The people which sat in the darkness saw a great light; and to them which sat in the region and shadow of death light did spring up." I wish to help you to realize the fact that we then enjoy this wide diffusion of the principles of morality and kindness, because Christ, the Son of Righteousness arose, and now for nearly 1900 years His moral influence has been penetrating and gradually affecting the world's thought. This enlightenment is by no means complete yet. It is still going on.

1. Contrast the opinions prevailing among men at the time Christ came, with the principles He laid down concerning our duty to God. True moral integrity and conscientious living was unknown. What would you expect when in the Roman empire, State dictated conscience to the individual; the individual had no right to a conscience; conception of heathen gods was simply projections and personifications of passions of the human heart. As gods, so people. Therefore society was a scene of mutual distrust and

hatred, refined deceptions, wicked amusements, gluttonous debaucheries, sanguinary cruelty, and the most corrupt and widespread sensuality. Seneca says : " All places are full of crimes and vices. Men strive in a sort of horrid competition in iniquity. Nor are crimes committed secretly. They walk before your eyes. To such a degree has wickedness been public and become strong in the breasts of all, that innocence is I cannot say even rare—it has ceased altogether to exist." The ruins of Pompeii, with their relics and frescoes, testify to the corruption of those days; the reigns of Tiberius and Nero—the very embodiments of sensuality, cruelty and of every vice ; the enjoyment of the populace, men and women over the sickening conflicts of thousands of gladiators. And what were the homes of those days? Alas ! there was no such thing as home. The word " family " to the ear of a Roman meant a multitude of idle, corrupt and corrupting slaves, kept in subjection by the lash, ready for any treachery and reeking with every vice. It meant a despot who could kill his slaves when they were aged, and expose his children when they were born ; it meant matrons among whom virtue was rare and divorce frequent; . it meant children spectators from their infancy of insolence and cruelty and servility and sin. But the new faith while it sanctioned the authority of parents, checked their despotism ; it made marriage sacred and indissoluable ; it encircled the position of womanhood with all that was pure and divine and tender in the name of mother and wife. For families in which, like sheltered flowers, spring up all that is purest and sweetest in human lives; for marriage exalted to almost sacramental dignity; for all that circle of heavenly blessings which result from a common self-sacrifice; for the beautiful unison of noble manhood, stainless womanhood, joyful infancy, and uncontaminated youth. In a word, for all there is of divinity and sweetness in the one word *home*. For this, to an extent which we can hardly realize, we are indebted to Christianity alone. If any one wants to read a brief but plain and firm portrayal of that heathen society in Christ's day, let him read Romans 1st. A master sketch confirmed thus by secular history. The Jews were somewhat better, perhaps, but with them ceremonialism, sacrifices offered, no change of will, asceticism, morbid withdrawal from men, clearly indicated that the Pagan and Jewish world sat in darkness, but yet Christ came like the sun into this moral midnight. He spoke of God's holiness requiring purity and righteousness. He reiterated and unfolded the divine law, showed how it extended to the heart. His beatitudes, shafts of morning light; and not in word only, but in deed also. He embodied this pure and heavenly morality, in which men have never been able to find a flaw, and which impresses the more we ponder it.

II. But if so as to personal integrity, how as to duty to our fellow man? Here is, also, the greatest possible contrast between Christ's teachings and spirit on the one hand, and the prevailing opinions of His day on the other. When he came the world was utterly and outrageously selfish. Principal nations each regarded themselves so superior to foreigners that foreigners were considered as made for their benefit. Thus the Greeks regarded and despised all others, even Egyptians and Romans, as barbarians. Humanity, only human race or culture. Socrates thanked the gods daily that he was man, not beast; Greek, not barbarian. The Romans considered all others foes. The Jews thought they had the exclusive possession of Jehovah's promises; they thought God created the world on their account. Selfishness everywhere. No charity, but contempt for the poor and suffering multitudes. The rich did not think of building asylums, hospitals, orphanages; but the strong everywhere derided and oppressed the weak. Pity and gentleness were almost unknown, and disinherited love in the Christian sense, a stranger to the earth. How like the sunrise then came Christ preaching the truth, that God is the Father of all men and that all men are brothers. What a world of fresh and glorious light poured in when He said, "I am annointed to preach the gospel to the poor. Come unto me all ye that labor and are heavy laden." No class or condition were exempt; all were invited to draw nigh and receive the blessing they needed. Where will you find such principles of self-sacrifice as were embodied in Christ and illustrated in His every action and word? You can readily see how Christ could not have been the outgrowth of the age in which He lived.

> "From heaven He came, of heaven He spoke,
> To heaven He lead His followers' way;
> Dark clouds of gloomy night He broke
> Unveiling an immortal day."

# CHAPTER VI.

## THE GOOD EFFECTS OF CHRISTIANITY THE BEST EVIDENCE OF ITS DIVINE ORIGIN.

(EXTRACTS.)

All candid readers of the Bible readily perceive that it teaches true piety toward God, and strict morality in all human relations. "For all scripture is given by inspiration of God, and is profitable for doctrine, for reproof, for correction, for instruction in righteousness." And it has produced the best moral effects in improving and reforming nations and individuals. "In the judgment of candid observers," as a writer has observed, "it has changed the condition of those nations which have embraced it, and introduced a degree of knowledge, of morality, of civilization and of domestic happiness, of which there was no experience before its appearance."

It has humanized the general manners, and produced many individual examples of virtue, to which no other religion can present a parallel. It has clearly shown itself to be a safe and effective guide for men in all their relations to God and each other. Hence we may safely and with confidence appeal to the good moral effects of the gospel for evidence of its truth. In confirmation of this proposition I will here quote an extract from a forcible and popular author. Says this writer:

"The effects of the gospel is the evidence to which the sacred writers appeal for its inspired truth as a divine revelation. The effect is seen, first, in the conversion of sinners, to God of all classes, ages and conditions, when all human means of reforming them have utterly failed. Second, in its giving them peace, joy and happiness, and in transforming their lives. Third, in making them different men—in making the drunkard sober, the thief honest, the licentious pure, the profane reverent, the indolent industrious, the harsh and unkind gentle and kind, and the wretched happy. Fourth, in its diffusing a mild and pure influence over the laws and customs of society, and in promoting human happiness everywhere."

And in regard to this evidence to which the sacred writers appeal, we may observe, first, that it is a kind of evidence which any one may examine, and which no one can reasonably deny. It does not need labored, abstruse argumentation, but it is everywhere in society. Every man in Christian countries, has witnessed the effects of the gospel in reforming the vicious, and no one can deny that it has this power. Second, it is a mighty display of the power of God. There is no more striking exhibition of his power over mind than in a revival of religion. There is nowhere more manifest demonstration of his presence than when in such a revival the proud are humbled, the profane are awed, the blasphemer is silenced, and the profligate, the abandoned, and the immoral are converted unto God and are led as lost sinners to the same cross and find the same peace. Third, the gospel has thus evidenced from age to age that it is from God.

Every converted sinner furnishes such a demonstration; every instance where it produces peace, hope and joy, shows that it is from heaven. In every generation God furnishes us a firm and solid demonstration that the Christian religion, which demands our belief, is from heaven. The power of God attends His inspired truth in transforming His people everywhere, and is a demonstration that is irresistible to every intelligent and really candid mind, that the religion of our Lord was not originated by mere human device or plan, but by Almighty God himself. And his power is manifest in changing the depraved heart of man from sin to holiness; in overcoming the strong propensities of our nature to sin; in subduing the soul, and making the sinner a new creature in Jesus Christ. Every Christian has thus, in his own experience, furnished demonstration that the religion which he loves is from God and not from man.

Man without divine grace would not subdue these sins, and man could not so entirely transform the soul. And although the unlearned Christian may not be able to investigate all the evidences of religion, although he cannot meet and refute all the objections of science or philosophy (falsely, so called), although he may be greatly perplexed by the seeming discrepancies of the sacred record, or by the seeming contradictions of new developments in science, yet he may have the witness of the Holy Spirit in his own experience that he is a renewed man; he may have the fullest proof that he loves God, that he is different from what he was once, and that all has been accomplished by the religion of Christ. The blind man that was made to see by the Saviour, might have been wholly unable to tell how his eyes were opened, and unable to meet all the cavils of those who might doubt it, or all the cunning and subtle objections of physiologists, but one thing he certainly could not doubt, that whereas he was blind he then saw.

A man may have no doubt that the sun shines, that the wind blows, that the tides rise, that the blood flows in the veins, that the flowers bloom, and that this could not be except it was from God, while he may have no power to explain these facts—no power to meet the objections and cavils of those who might choose to embarrass him.

So men may know that their hearts are changed by the Holy Ghost, giving efficacy to the inspired word of God. And it is on this ground that humble and unlearned Christians, in all ages of our world, chiefly depend for the most satisfactory evidence of the absolute truth of the Christian religion. They know they love God, and delight in his service in life, and they know that on such evidence of His truth they may safely trust the redemption of their souls in death, with the assurance of rising to newness of life in the morning of the final resurrection.

"The revelations of prophecy," observes a writer whom I quote at length, in closing, "are facts which exhibit the divine omniscience. So long as Babylon is in heaps, so long as Ninevah lies empty, void and waste; so long as Egypt is the basest of kingdoms;

so long as Tyre is a place for the spreading of nets in the midst of the sea; so long as Israel is scattered among all nations; so long as Jerusalem is trodden under foot of the Gentiles; so long as the great empires of the world march on in their predicted course, —so long we have proof that one omniscient Mind dictated that Book, and 'prophecy came not in old time by the will of man.'

"We call this Bible a book, but here are sixty-six different books, written by thirty or forty different men. A man may say, 'I do not believe in the book of Esther.' Well, what of that? We have sixty-five others left. What will you do with them? A man says, 'I find fault with this chapter or with that.' Suppose you do? If you were on trial for murder, and had sixty-six witnesses against you, suppose you impeach one of them, there are sixty-five left; impeach another, and you still have sixty-four; impeach another, and you have sixty-three—enough to hang you up if you are guilty. Do you not see that you cannot impeach this Book unless you do it in detail? Each book bears its own witness, and stands by itself on its own merits; and yet each book is linked with all the rest. Blot out one, if you can. I am inclined to think it would be difficult to do this. This Book is built to stay together; it is inspired by one Spirit.

"The authorship of this Book is wonderful. Here are words written by kings, by emperors, by princes, by poets, by sages, by philosophers, by fishermen, by statesmen; by men learned in the wisdom of Egypt, educated in the schools of Babylon, trained up at the feet of rabbis in Jerusalem. It was written by men in exile, in the desert, and in shepherd's tents, in 'green pastures' and beside 'still waters.' Among its authors we find the fisherman, the tax-gatherer, the herdsman, the gatherer of sycamore fruit; we find poor men, rich men, statesmen, preachers, exiles, captains, legislators, judges—men of every grade and class. The authorship of this Book is wonderful beyond all other books.

"And what a book it is—filled with law, ethics, prophecy, poetry, history, genealogy, medicine, sanitary science, political economy. It contains all kinds of writing; but what a jumble it would be if sixty-six books were written in this way by ordinary men. Suppose, for instance, that we get sixty-six medical books written by thirty or forty different doctors of various schools, believers in allopathy, homeopathy, hypathy, and all the other opathies, bind them all together, and then undertake to doctor a man according to that book! What man would be fool enough to risk the results of practicing such a system of medicine? Or, suppose you get thirty-five editors writing treatises on politics, or thirty-five ministers writing books on theology, and then see if you can find any leather strong enough to hold the books together when they have got through.

"But again, it required fifteen hundred years to write this Book, and the man who wrote the closing pages of it had no communication with the man who commenced it. How did these men, writing independently, produce such a book? Other books get out of date when they are ten or twenty years old: But this Book lives on through the ages, and keeps abreast of the mightiest thought and intellect of every age.

"Again, I conclude that this book has in it the very breath of God, from the effect it produces upon men. There are men who study philosophy, astronomy, geology, geography, and mathematics, but did you ever hear a man say, 'I was an outcast, a wretched inebriate, a disgrace to my race, and a nuisance in the world, until I began to study mathematics, and learned the multiplication table, and then turned my attention to geology, got me a little hammer, and knocked off the corners of the rocks and studied the formation of the earth; but since that time I have been happy as the day is long; I feel like singing all the time, my soul is full of triumph and peace; and health and blessing has come to my desolate home once more.' Did you ever hear a man ascribe his redemption and salvation from intemperance and sin and vice to the multiplication table, or the science of mathematics or geology? But I can bring you not one man, or two, or ten, but men by the thousand who will tell you, 'I was wretched; I was lost; I broke my poor old mother's heart; I beggared my family; my wife was broken-hearted and dejected; my children fled from the sound of their father's footstep; I was ruined, reckless, helpless, homeless, hopeless, until I heard the words of that Book!' And he will tell you the very words which fastened on his soul. It may be it was, 'Come unto Me, all ye that labor and are heavy laden, and I will give you rest;' perhaps it was, 'Behold the Lamb of God, which taketh away the sin of the world;' It may have been, 'God so loved the world that he gave his only begotten Son, that whosoever believeth in him should not perish but have everlasting life.' He can tell you what the very word was which saved his soul. And since that word entered his heart, he will tell you that hope has dawned upon his vision; that joy has inspired his heart; and that his mouth is filled with grateful song. He will tell you that the blush of health has come back to his poor wife's faded cheek; that the old hats have vanished from the windows of his desolate home; that his rags have been exchanged for good clothes; that his children run to meet him when he comes; that there is bread on his table, fire on his hearth, and comfort in his dwelling. He will tell you all that, and he will tell you that this Book has done the work. Now, this Book is working just such miracles, and is doing it every day. If you have any other book that will do such work as this, bring it along. The work needs to be done; if you have the book that will do it, for Heaven's sake bring it out. But for the present, while we are waiting for you, as we know this Book *will* do the work we propose to use it until we can get something better. And the best thing for us to do is to bring out the word of God, and let the 'sword of the Spirit' prove its own power, as it pierces 'even to the dividing assunder of soul and spirit.'

"Suppose, for example, all the good people of any community should try the Bible, say for a single year. Suppose you start now, and say, 'We have heard about that Book, and now we will begin and practice its teachings just one year.' What would be the result? There would be no lying, no stealing, no selling rum, no getting drunk, no tattling, no mischief-making, no gossiping, no vice or debauchery. Every man would be a good man, every woman a good woman; every man would be a good husband, father, or brother, every woman a good wife, mother, or sister; every one in the community would be peaceable; there would be no brawls, no quarrels, no fights, no lawsuits; lawyers would almost starve to death; doctors would have light practice, and plenty of time to hoe their gardens; courts would be useless, jails and lockups empty, almshouses cleaned out of their inmates, except a few old stagers left over from the past generation; taxes would be reduced three-fourths, hard times would trouble nobody—all would be well-dressed and well cared for. It would raise the price of real estate twenty-five per cent in six months; taxes would come down, property would go up, and good people from far and near would want to move into town, and nobody who was worth having there would want to move out. And this would be the direct result of reading and *obeying this Book.* Now, if a book will do that for a community, what kind of a book is it? Is such a book the Lord's book or the devil's book? It seems to me that a book that will do such works as that, must be the Book of God, inspired by the very breath of the Almighty. The Book is its own witness. It bears its own fruits and tells its own story."

# CHAPTER VII.

## THE FALSE PHILOSOPHY AND DEMORALIZING INFLUENCE OF INFIDELITY PROVE THAT IT MUST BE UNTRUE.

While the good effect of Bible truths proves it to be inspired of God, the false philosophy of infidelity, and its demoralizing effects, show that it must be untrue.

Nothing can be more certain, maintains the infidel, than that no human being can by any possibility control his thought. We are in this world—we see, we hear, we feel, we taste; and everything in nature makes an impression upon the brain, and that wonderful something, enthroned there with these materials, weaves what we call thought, and the brain can no more help thinking than the heart can help beating. The blood pursues its old accustomed round without our will. The heart beats without asking leave of us, and the brain thinks in spite of all we can do. This being true, no human being can justly be held responsible for his thought any more than for the beating of his heart, any more more than for the course pursued by the blood, any more than for breathing air.

"That falsehood," observes a writer, "shot President Garfield. If it were the truth, it would be a full and complete justification of every murder, rape, arson, wife-beating, child-torturing, and of every crime that has been committed since time began. We are not afraid of the effects of such a preposterous falsehood on the minds of mature and thinking men and women—those who know and feel their responsibility to God and their fellow-men—but more deadly moral poison was never put into so small a shape for the minds of the immature and those who seek an excuse for the gratification of devilish propensities. A man is as much the master of his brain as he is of his premises. He is just as guilty—nay, much more guilty—if he permits an evil thought to fester and corrupt in his soul, as he is if he permit open sewers and dead animals and rotting vegetables to lie in his cellar, and poison his family to death. It is his duty to *clean them out*. If an evil passion shows its germ in his mind, he cannot let it spread and grow till it culminates in murder or adultery, and then say he is not responsible for it. If he does not uproot it and cast it out, and plant the seed of all good thoughts in its place, he will, if he gets his deserts, be hung in this world and damned in the next. That doctrine lies at the bottom of the infidel philosophy. In just so far as it is accepted, to that extent will all moral restraints be taken off the minds and consciences of men. It takes no heed of deadly consequences."

It says, "I am not responsible for my thoughts or their outcome."

It seems that the speculative infidelity of men must have paralyzed and stupified their minds, when their theory constrains them to deny their free agency and responsibility. Who in the exercise of ordinary reason, does not know that if two silver dollars were offered him, as near alike as possible in every particular, that he is perfectly free to choose either as a present from me, or to decline the present entirely. Thus his consciousness testifies to his free agency. And whose moral nature can be so obtuse and insensible as to feel that he is neither guilty for deliberate murder, nor to be commended for generous acts of beneficence?

When skeptics, in justification of their speculative theory of unbelief, deny their intellectual and moral nature, and are not blameworthy either for their unbelief of moral truth or their sinful conduct, which is its result, they must be greatly at fault. And God says of them: "Because they received not the love of the truth that they might be saved, he shall send them strong delusion that they should believe a lie, that they all might be damned who believe not the truth but had pleasure in unrighteousness."

Every man of sound mind, in the exercise of his reason, must know that he is not the irresponsible subject of arbitrary *fate*, but his consciousness and his conscience must both convince him that he is absolutely a *free agent*, responsible for all his deliberate, voluntary acts and intentions, both to the civil and divine law, and to society, and to Almighty God, his final Judge, for all his moral and religious or wicked conduct. Hence it appears obvious to all fair minded and candid men, that "every one of us shall give account of himself to God." It is reasonable, therefore, that "he that believeth shall be saved, and he that believeth not shall be damned."

# CHAPTER VIII.

## EXPERIMENTAL EVIDENCE OF THE TRUTH OF CHRISTIANITY.

(EXTRACTS.—DOING AND KNOWING.)

The Lord Jesus Christ has said, "If any man will do his will, he shall know of the doctrine, whether it be of God."

But does any objector say, "I must know the doctrine before I begin to practice it?" I reply this is unreasonable. And in its support I ask attention to the following extracts and considerations:

"If any man will do his will he shall know of the doctrine," said Christ. "But that," answers the doubter, "is unreasonable. That reverses the natural order. I must know the doctrine before I begin to practice it. You ask me to commit myself to a system of religion many of whose principles I do not understand. That is absurd."

Let us see. Perhaps this demand of Christ is not so irrational after all. It may be that men are constantly acting on the same principle in other affairs.

The art of speaking rests upon the science of grammar or rhetoric. But children always learn to talk before they study grammar. Would our objector insist that his baby must take a thorough course of Gould-Brown before he learned to talk? Would he pronounce it absurd in this case that practice should precede doctrine?

Every art is based upon science. The art consists of rules and methods, the science of laws and principles; the art is practical, the science is theoretical. And almost always the practice comes before the theory.

When, therefore, Christ says, "Do and you shall know," he lays down for the divine education a method which the most intelligent modern teachers have found it necessary to adopt. Religion is an art—the art of holy living. Theology is the science which underlies the art. And it is just as reasonable to ask a man to begin to practice religion before he fully understands theology, as it is to ask him to begin to practice any other art before he comprehends the corresponding science.

The inductive method in philosophy, which all our scientists in these days insist upon as the only valid method, requires us to collect our facts first and then draw reason from them. We are not allowed to develop our theories out of our own consciousness, and then see if we cannot find facts to fit them. We must first know what is, and then try to find what it means. Now this is precisely Christ's demand. Religion is for every man a concern intensely individual. The essence of it is submission to God and dependence on His grace. It consists largely of acceptance from him of help in our struggles with sin and in our endeavors to live righteously. It promises us support under suffering, comfort in sorrow, and a good hope in the hour of death.

All the doctrines of the Christian religion bear directly upon these practical issues. Now, how can any man find out whether the doctrines are true unless he will put them to the test of practice. The facts which establish the doctrines are facts which he must find in his own experience. He cannot explore the minds of other men. He may be able to judge, somewhat imperfectly, by observing their conduct, whether they do receive this divine aid or not; but there is only one absolutely certain method of knowing whether there is answer to prayer, whether there is solace in affliction, whether the strength and peace of God are given to them that ask—and that is by trying. When a man has collected out of his own experience facts enough upon which to base an induction, then he will know of the doctrine. He can never know in any other way. And when he refuses to take this method of finding out, and insists that he must be certain of the results before he makes the experiment, he is as unreasonable as one who, having always lived in a dungeon, should insist upon knowing for himself that the light and heat of the sun were pleasant before he would go out of his cellar into the daylight.

Religion is prayer. When it was said of Saul of Tarsus "Behold, he prayeth," it was meant that he had entered upon the religious life. There were many things that he did not understand, but he had submitted his will to God and was seeking for light. So any man who sincerely prays to God with submission of the will and consecration of the life is a religious man. That is the only way to become religious. One who desires to do the will of God must know what is the will of God. He will find that out by praying, as Saul did: " Lord, what wilt thou have me to do?" Whoever will offer this prayer in simplicity and sincerity day by day, and will accept such light as he can get from the study of God's truth and use of his own reason, will quickly find that his worst doubts are vanishing. There may be some subjects yet that he cannot quite master, but nothing over which his faith will stumble If God is infinite, it is not likely that all the truth about Him can be put into a definition. But they who do his will shall be made more and more certain, in their earnest search for wisdom, that to the knowledge of divine truth, as to every other sort of knowledge, obedience is the royal road.

Whatever may be the skill of the teaching, the prime condition of knowledge in moral things is in the heart itself. If in all the lower forms of feelings and the truths belonging to them, experience must be the basis of knowledge, how much more should we expect it to be so in the range of the higher moral faculties! We come to the Bible from the analogies of nature, with the expectation of such a teaching.

Now look, for a moment, at some of the truths which Christ was wont to teach. Earliest, was repentance for sin. Whatever explanations may be given to the understanding of the nature of repentance, they will be invalid and obscure until the feeling itself interprets them. That grief for sin is not all grief, but is tempered with trust, and love, and sorrow, without fear for the future, but full of regrets for the past; that says "Against Thee and Thee only have I sinned," as if nothing else was worth thinking of in comparison with the fact that God had been offended—who shall know this, except through the experience of it? There may be a suggestive flavor of it in generous hearts, in the nobler forms of earthly love; but only in a Christian's experience do we know its full disclosures. Those that have felt it interpret your words when you speak of it with great heart-swellings; but to those who have not known it, your words of interpretation are but as sounding brass or a tinkling cymbal.

The reality and the joy of entire submission to God; the sense of the Divine worthiness; the disclosure of the beauty of holiness; heart-gladness on account of God's supremacy; a glorying in the thought of His universal Fatherhood; an unspeakable satisfaction in the conviction of His love toward us, of our adoption through it, of our sympathetic union with Him, of our co-operative life in this world and of our union with Him in immortality; that reverence which prostrates us before the grandeur and purity of his Being; the stranger mystery of that feeling which inspires the soul with a sense of honor and glory in the act of its humiliation before God; that wonderful experience which causes the heart to scorn as an indignity, and reject as a monstrous wrong, the humbling of itself before human beings, but which bows it down with eager willingness and gladness before God, and fills it with the divinest sense of the greatness that there is in childlike simplicity and Christlike humility; the sense of God's presence; the perception of God in the work of His hands in nature; the supernal beauty of this world when to faith it is transfused with the Spirit of God.

By what possible explanations or formulas can these truths be taught? How shall one find them unless they spring out of his own heart? Yet less can be taught of that wondrous truth which is the blossom of the whole creation—*Love*. Our experiences of it one toward another, are but its lower leaves. What is it when God solicits it and nourishes it in the human soul? What is it when it is the harmony of all the faculties of our nature, and, inspired by God, it takes hold upon him as the all-worthy object of its supreme strength? These, thank God, are experiences possible here; but they must precede knowing. Words and letters will not teach them.

We ask no favor, no grace, but only that you be willing to accept religious truth according to its nature, as you do all others.

I stand in the door of Christian life, and declaim of the untold gladness of love, hope and faith; of the joys of humility, of manly self renunciation, of the peace and rest which devotion breathes upon the soul, of the solace of penitence—the profound joy of gratitude. Do you demand that such truths shall be *proved*, as if they were intellectual propositions?

Will you reason upon a fact of consciousness, as if it were an outward fact of matter? The foundation of thinking in respect to truths of moral consciousness is *feeling*. As no man can spin until he has either cotton or wool, so no man can think until he has the staple from which thought is twisted. Feeling is the wool out of which the thread and fabric of thought, in many departments of Truth, are made. And though I do not despise the thread or the fabric, I recognize the fact that all understanding of moral truth must be based upon moral experience.

When men come to the Gospel, they must come to it as little children; that is, they must come and ask *what it is*, and not to pronounce what it *ought to be*. For a great while the world undertook to establish natural science by teaching what they supposed ought to be the structure of nature. They found out nothing of the composition of air or fluids; they discovered nothing of the qualities of water or fire; they made themselves acquainted with neither geology nor chemistry. It was not until, instead of arrogantly measuring nature upon their own preconceived theories, they humbled themselves and sat at the feet of God in nature, that there grew up a school of truth broad and wise.

The same fact exists in relation to moral truth. There never can be a teaching to a mind that assumes to know beforehand the truth to be taught. And our business is to ask, "What is truth?" If the scientific man demands that we shall preach the Gospel of Christ and the truths of religious experience, in such a way that they shall be mathematically demonstrated, he demands that which is simply impossible. I have, however, both heard and seen printed, the declaration that we are bound to give a mathematical demonstration of the truths which we advocate. I regard the absurdity of this as not one whit less than would be that of asking for a pound of love or two ounces of pity. What! apply physical measures to moral qualities? Just as much as mathematical reasonings! No, physical measures and mathematical reasonings are applicable to material substances only. And those processes of teaching which belong to matter are impertinent when demanded in the presentation of moral or affectionate truths.

The philosophical reasoner who resolves all truths from their living forms into abstractions, travels right away from the nutritious form of truth. An abstraction of intellect is never a living truth. It is but an artificial creation. There may be good uses for abstractions. But they belong to the school, the training room. Religious truths chiefly concern themselves with human duties and dispositions. The Gospel is not a system of philosophical truths, but a guide book of practical life—a prescription for the heart and conduct.

Hence this teaching indicates, in the clearest manner, what is the substance of Christianity. It is the life of the soul according to a Divine method, that constitutes the religion of Christ. The Bible, the church, the ministry, and doctrines and precepts, are all instruments, and the truth to which they minister is always in the living consciousness of the individual or else it has no existence at all.

Christ says, "By their fruits ye shall know them." And I aver that that man who is at peace with God through love to men; who not merely says he loves God and men, but blossoms all over with love; who wherever he goes is fragrant with Divine gifts; whose face is ever radiant with goodness; who carries gentleness and sweetness in the house, and in the street, and everywhither—I aver that that man is right.

And I aver that if a man will do the will of God, he shall learn in that way, whether the teaching of Christ is of God or not. Let a man prostrate himself before God; let him begin to ask direction of God, and wish to be directed by him; let him take fundamental truths of the Gospel, and attempt, earnestly and perseveringly, to conform his life to them—let a man do these things, and not only will he become a Christian, but he will touch all the great doctrines of theology.

Suppose, for instance, that a man desires to be convinced of one's inability to correct his own life. Let him attempt to practice the command, "Thou shalt love the Lord thy God with all thy heart, and with all thy soul, and with all thy strength, and with all thy mind, and thy neighbor as thyself," and if he does not come to a sense of his inability to do it, and of his need of Divine help, his experience will be different from that of any man I ever knew.

Suppose that a man desires to be convinced of the sinfulness of the heart. You say to him, "The Bible says it is sinful." He says, "I do not believe the Bible." "You ought to." "Well, I do not." You can get no further with him. Or, if he professes to believe the Bible, and is ingenious in an argument, you may quote to him passage after passage, and he will evade them all, by saying they are relative to such and such things which have no relation to the doctrine you are endeavoring to prove. He will go through the whole Bible, like a plow, throwing your citations aside, and leaving an iron track behind him.

When I come across such a man, I say to him, "Do you not believe that, being sustained by God, you owe constant obedience and reverence to him?" He says "That is natural teaching—I believe that." "Do you not believe that you ought to obey the command, 'Thou shalt love God supremely, and thy neighbor as thyself'?" "Yes—that is reasonable." "Well, then, will you undertake to conform your life to it for the space of one week?" "I have no objection to that." So he begins on Monday to try to live in such a way that in everything he does, love to God and love to his neighbor shall predominate. He succeeds very well so long as nothing comes up to disturb his equanimity; but the moment worldly influences touch his pride, it breaks out like a tiger; and he says to himself, "Hold! hold! Pride. Thou art to love God and thy neighbor." Pride flashes and thunders and throws out cinders, determined not to be governed by any such law. When this eruption is over with, the man says, "I will make another trial," and he goes to New York, and there his selfishness is aroused; and before the sun goes down he finds himself striving as greedily for gain as other men.

And, when, at the end of the week, he reviews his

conduct during the period allotted for the undertaking, he finds that it has been characterized by nothing else so little as a spirit of love; and he says, "I do not believe it is possible for me to love God supremely and my neighbor as myself. I have tried to do it for a whole week, and I have not had a single conception of God; and as for loving all men, I cannot do it. There is not a thing in me that does not rebel against it."

That is just what I have been preaching to the man. He has acknowledged the very thing of which I desired to convince him—namely, that all the faculties of the human soul are sinful, and refuse to let a man live aright. He has become convinced of both the doctrine of dependence upon God, and the doctrine of human sinfulness. And let him go on in the same way, step by step, attempting to carry out in his life all the precepts of the Gospel, and he will by-and-by become convinced of the doctrine of regeneration, the doctrine of adoption, the doctrine of justification, the doctrine of sanctification, and all the other fundamental doctrines of Christianity. Let a man attempt to live, and succeed in living, according to the spirit of Christ, and his doubts will be removed in regard to the whole Gospel scheme. "If any man will do his will, he shall know of the doctrine, whether it be of God, or whether I speak of myself." A Christian experience includes in it the essential facts of the Gospel of the Lord Jesus Christ.

I avoid reasoning with honest persons in respect to Christianity, not because I undervalue reasoning, but because I think there is a better way of presenting the truth to them. I was brought up in a school where argumentation was as natural as walking, but my pastoral experience has been such as to convince me that that is not the best means to employ for removing men's doubts on the subject of religion. My direction to any man that wants to come to Christ is, " Begin to be a Christian." If he says, " I do not know about it," I say, " Begin, and you will find out." I put him at once upon the practice of Christianity, as the shortest way of answering his objections. The moment he has the life of Christ in him, it will begin to remove them out of the way: and it will do more in a single moment than you can do in years and years by hard debate and argument. And when the work is done in this way, it does not have to be done the second time; for with reference to that which a man has learned by experience, he never says, " I do not believe."

So, as long as a man's soul is under the dominion of pride, and selfishness, and worldly will, there is nothing in him that will accept the truth; but the moment the warmth of the Divine Spirit pours in upon him, his nature begins to melt and flow down, and his heart begins to soften, and there is fructification, the results of which are seen in his life.

This is the parable of Christ: A sower went forth to sow. Some seeds fell by the wayside, some on rock, and some on good ground. Those which fell on prepared soil sprang up and brought forth much fruit. And where a heart is in such a state that it can be reached by Christian truth, that truth springs up and brings forth fruit in abundance to the glory of God.

If you would learn of Christ, go directly to Christ himself. If you want to know whether the words he spoke are true or not, attempt to put into daily practice in your disposition, in your heart, in your deeds, what he taught by the four evangelists. If I had a man that was an infidel, who had an honest spot in him, and I wanted to convert him to Christianity, I would shut him up in a house with just four rooms in it, I would turn the lock on him, and I would say to him, "You shall abide here till you make yourself acquainted with these four rooms. The first is Matthew; the second, opening out of that, is Mark; the third, opening out of that, is Luke; and the fourth, high out of that crystal roof, in those evanishing pictures far above the reach of the strongest and furthest-seeing eye, is John, fit revelator. Here are your teachers and lessons. You shall study no other book; and these you shall study by practicing what is in them. Take the teachings of Christ which they contain, and practice them for a time, and then, from the experience resulting from practice, you shall know of the truth of Christ, whether it be of God or not." I do not believe any honest man, if put through such a course of training as that, could fail to come out a Christian.

May God give you honesty, and induce you to put in practice the truths of religion, as the shortest way of ascertaining their verity.

# CHAPTER IX.

## THE CONSISTENT CHRISTIAN LIFE THE BEST FOR TIME AND THE SAFEST FOR ETERNITY.

The strictly consistent Christian, in the opinion of believers and unbelievers, the righteous and the wicked, aims habitually to be and do just right in all his relations to God and man, and by so doing promote his own happiness. He studies diligently the revelations God has made of his perfect character in his works and word, that he may love him supremely, and worship him in spirit and in truth, so that he may be "changed into the same image, from glory to glory, even as by the spirit of the Lord." He is deeply penitent for his sins in thought, word and deed, he trusts in the atonement of Jesus Christ for pardon, seeks divine grace in resisting temptation, and strives to imitate his Saviour's perfect and holy example so that he may "walk in all the commandments and ordinances of the Lord blameless." And in proportion as such a Christian shall succeed in obeying all the requirements of his Maker, will he enjoy a sense of the divine approval and the approval of his own conscience, so as to promote his highest and most permanent enjoyment in the present life.

In proportion as he obeys the physical, intellectual and moral laws of his Creator, will he promote his own general health and cheerfulness. The industry, economy and prudence, inseparably connected with the consistent Christian life, will commonly be rewarded with a comfortable competency of property, so as to save him from distressing anxiety concerning his needful support.

His uniform benevolence, kindness, integrity, and strict uprightness in all his relations with his fellow-men, will commonly ensure their confidence and respect, so that he will enjoy a good measure of their sympathy and approval.

Such a Christian will endeavor by the assistance of divine grace to submit promptly and readily to the unavoidable afflictions of life, and in the prospect of death will commonly enjoy bright hopes of perfect blessedness of heaven. In this way it appears that the consistent Christian excels the devotee of worldliness and sin, in securing the greater benefits of the present life. And if it is possible that his high hopes of an immortality of blessedness beyond the grave shall not be realized, he has been a great and surpassing gainer of the real blessings which he has enjoyed in the present world, over those who have pursued a life of sinful indulgence and neglect of true and saving piety.

But if it shall prove true, as he believes, (and no man can know the contrary) that " our Saviour,

Jesus Christ, hath abolished death and brought life and immortality to light, through the gospel," how inconceivably joyous and ecstatic must be his eternal felicity in the future "world of durable riches and righteousness." And if "it is appointed unto men once to die, but after this the judgment," and "if we must all appear before the judgment seat of Christ that every one may receive the things done in his body, according to that he hath done, whether it be good or bad;" and if "the wicked shall go away into eternal punishment and the righteous into life eternal," what mind can conceive or language describe the misery of the worldly and sinful, who neglected religion in time, and lost their souls for eternity! With this view of the possibility of an immortal existence of the human soul in the world of just retribution, is it not safest to live and die a consistent Christian? Does not every real Christian know that when he passes from darkness to light, from the bondage of sin to a life of liberty and holiness, by the washing of regeneration and renewing of the Holy Ghost, he became a better and happier man and more hopeful in anticipation of a blessed eternity?

Therefore, may he not wisely rest satisfied with such facts in his own experience, although he may be unable clearly and logically to refute the multiplied cavils of unbelief and the sophistries of skepticism? Do not all men reasonably expect the true followers of Christ to be better men than the mere devotees of this sinful world, however infidel, heretical or superstitious they may be themselves, while they common-

# THE TRUTH OF THE BIBLE PROVED.

ly expect those who apostatize from their Christian profession to be more immoral in their lives?

And does not this fact show, that they regard the consistent Christian life the best for time (and if there be a future existence) the safest for eternity? And in the hour of death, was it ever known that any one ever regretted that he had lived a consistent Christian life? But in that awful hour how many have manifested great distress in view of their past unbelief and neglect of religion? Certainly "their rock is not as our rock, even our enemies themselves being judges." " But godliness is profitable unto all things, having promise of the life that now is, and of that which is to come."

# CHAPTER X.

## RESPONSIBILITY FOR BELIEF.

Upon a man's belief or unbelief of the Bible, with its precious doctrines, is suspended momentous results. " He that believeth, and is baptized, shall be saved ; but he that believeth not, shall be damned."

Although men are greatly influenced in their religious beliefs by their constitutional tendencies and educational circumstances, they cannot doubt or discredit God's truth, pertaining to the Christian religion, without fearful peril to their eternal welfare. If they disbelieve God's natural law by partaking of arsenic, although it may appear as innocent as powdered chalk, they must suffer the dangerous consequences.

Why is this? Is not God good? Yea, verily. But his goodness leads him to teach men that for disbelief in the effects of things natural, they are responsible to him, and must suffer fearful penalties. Hence it seems reasonable that men should be responsible to God for their religious belief, because their belief controls their moral conduct.

It is generally admitted that a man's religious belief is a good index to his present character and future actions. "For as he thinketh in his heart, so is he." "Take away the fear of punishment," as a writer has observed, "and present the occasion to him who believes that stealing is justifiable, and no man of sense is surprised that the belief rules the life." The mass of criminal convicts believe themselves, for some reason, to have been justifiable in the perpetration of their crimes. So long as they thus believe, every orderly citizen knows that they are dangerous to society.

A man's creed, it is very plain, embodies his moral principles. But if he who believes viciously acts correctly, it is owing to causes foreign from his real character, and there is no proper ground of praise or blame in what he does. It is true that decided unbelievers are sometimes good citizens, but it is not the natural result of their unbelief; for no code of morals admits of fortuitous virtue. Furthermore, it is obvious that men are responsible for the thorough pursuit, and impartial appreciation of evidence in support of truth.

For it is plain that all enlightened belief depends upon the evidence which the mind apprehends, and not that which exists but is not perceived. Therefore, we are bound to search dilligently for the best evidence of which the nature of the case admits, and then weigh the evidence or testimony with strict candor and impartiality.

"Why," as one inquires, "do not those whose interests are opposed see the evidence alike which is presented in a Court of Justice?" Under the influence of biased feelings, men take only a partial view of the evidence submitted to them, while they study minutely all the circumstances deemed favorable to themselves, and to undervalue those of an opposite tendency; and this unfair appreciation produces a biased and incorrect belief, as certainly as if but one side had been adduced.

If from such considerations as these men are responsible to society in temporal affairs, is it not most reasonable that they should be responsible to God for their belief in eternal affairs? "If we receive the witness of men, the witness of God is greater." If erroneous belief is often injurious for this life, and often fatal, who can show that it will not be equally, or more so, in the life beyond the grave? If man's welfare now requires him to believe in the fixed laws of God's natural government, may it not be much more important that he should believe in the fixed laws of His moral government?

In the light of this subject we perceive why some men believe the Gospel, and others reject it, while the same evidence is in existence for the examination of both classes. When both are urged to believe the Gospel, and be converted, and imbibe the teachable spirit of little children in receiving its inspired intructions, one class searches dilligently and honestly for proofs in its support, as for hidden treasure, and believes with the heart unto righteousness, and is made wise unto salvation. The other in his perversity, neglects all real honest inquiries, "and for this cause God shall send them strong delusion, that they shall believe a lie, that they all might be damned who believe not the truth but had pleasure in unrighteousness."

"Finally," says Prof. Northrop, "let us amid all the excitement of the age, all the unrest of the gathering doubt and unbelief, stand firm in this confidence that Jesus Christ and this gospel are adapted to the needs of men. That which is necessary to men, men will ultimately come to have. This gospel is necessary to man as a social being, as a member of society. Why, without this gospel and without the future life, what would society be? If Lazarus received evil things and the rich man good things, and *if this life is all*, tell me why the Lazaruses combining should not take the good things from the rich men and use them for themselves in this life? You would if you were in their place; I would if I were in their place. It is the restraining power of the moral government of Almighty God, and the truth of His government as revealed in the revelation of Jesus Christ that is to be the salvation of the world, and to save it from the errors of socialism, and communism, and nihilism, if it is saved at all.

"But more than all, my friends, is this: Here all is pleasant; here the forces move on swiftly; the currents of life are easy; we are gathered here enjoying each other's faces; there is no sadness and no sorrow here. But that is not the whole of life. There are moments of sadness, especially moments when we stand by those dearer to us than our lives, and see them pass away by that mysterious process we call death. And when that hour comes, as come to every one of us it will, tell me, Oh, unbeliever, what comfort you can give in an hour like that? Tell me, Ingersoll, preaching infidelity through the country and robbing men of their last hope in that hour of agony, what words of consolation can you speak? And there is silence—silence that must be, silence even when hearts are breaking with anguish. And is there any voice in all the universe that comes to us with comfort save the single voice of our Saviour, Jesus Christ, 'who hath abolished death and hath brought life and immortality to light through the gospel?' 'I am the resurrection and the life; he that believeth in me, though he were dead, yet shall he live; and whosoever liveth and believeth in me shall never die.'

"Ah, this is comfort! 'For if we believe that Jesus died and rose again, even so them also which sleep in Jesus will God bring with Him.' And there comes through every heart, man and woman through all Christendom, when that hour comes, the longing for the blessed Lord. 'Oh, my Lord, my blessed Lord; I shall see the dear one I have lost, the lamb whom Thou hast taken to Thine own bosom.'

"Oh, ministers of God, preachers of the Gospel of Jesus Christ, lift up your standard even in this age, and bear it bravely forward. You are preaching to men, to men with hearts and feelings and affections. They will need the gospel which you preach. Go preach it then; be strong in the Lord; there is no discouragement that He has not foreseen, and which the voice of prophecy has not proclaimed; there is brightness ahead; bear on the banner, and the victory shall be the Lord's. For modern literature with its unbelief shall pass away; yea, 'Heaven and earth shall pass away, but my words,' saith the Lord, 'shall not pass away.'

"If Mr. Huxley thinks that it requires a robust faith to believe that man has any existence after death, we have a perfect right to think that it requires a more robust faith to believe that man has no existence after death. The greatest scholar I ever knew believed that death was but as the passage from one room to another, and when he died I have no doubt he realized that expectation. If there was nothing else to convince us of the future life, except the incompleteness of this, I would still believe in a future life; for, that a splendid mind, full of thought, full of the mature learning of years, should go out suddenly like the beasts that perish, and be no more, is beyond belief."

# CHAPTER XI.

## SINCERITY INSUFFICIENT.

### (EXTRACTS.)

The Bible is given for the promotion of godliness of life. It is admirably adapted to that end, and to make men happy hereafter, as well as good here. And the apostle Paul blames, by implication on the one side, those that neglect its truths wholly, and, on the other side, those that overzealously employ its truths for the promotion of something else besides godliness. It "is profitable for doctrine, for reproof, for correction, for instruction in righteousness, that"—this is the final end—"that the man of God may be perfect, thoroughly furnished unto all good works;" not unto all good belief—and yet he is to believe; not unto soundness of doctrine—and yet he is to be sound in doctrine. In other words, the apostle here shows that truth is important, but that it is a means to an end; and that the higher end is the godliness of a man's life; is piety and holiness. Truth is therefore an instrument for the production of that result.

Comprehensively, then, we may say that there are two things to be noticed: first, that the proper use and end of all religious knowledge is the promotion of good conduct and character; and secondly, that there is a definite and important relation between certain truths and certain results of truth. It is not indifferent what a man believes. The same fruits will not follow as well from one set of principles as from another. A man must believe right.

In the main this is the universal belief. Believing is the basis of all instruction and education. Every parent, every teacher, every moralist, as well as every preacher of righteousness, believes that human life and conduct will largely depend upon the things that men are taught to believe.

It is only when we come to moral truths, to religious teachings, that there has sprung up a very different impression; a strange heresy, indeed. For there is a popular impression that it makes no difference what a man believes, if he is only *sincere*. And this takes on many forms, and runs through a wide range of applications.

It is employed, for instance, to reduce all churches and all theologies to an equality. It is said that one faith, whether it be Catholic or Protestant, Mohammedan or Christian, is as good as another, so that it is sincerely held. Men say, " It makes no difference what a man believes if he is only sincere in his religion." To their mind, the belief of the poor Indian, the belief of the Chinese, and all the other beliefs in the world, from the highest to the lowest, are about the same. They think that being sincere is the great thing, and not the particular belief.

It is employed, also, to signify the equality of mere conventional morality, without any real religious feeling or faith of any kind, with spiritual and experimental religion. A prayerless, godless, worldly man, of an amiable turn, who conforms to the maxims of morality which exist in the community about him is wont to say, "I have no great deal of religion, and I do not trouble myself much about religious doctrines; but I believe in doing right, and, after all, it makes not so much difference, if a man is only sincere in what he does believe."

There is just enough truth in this phrase, in some of its applications, to make it plausable, and to give it currency. And so it has come to be a proverb.

No proverb could touch more points of important truth than this one, which says it makes no difference what a man believes, so that he is sincere. It touches the whole question of believing, and of the workings of the things believed.

As to its origin. How did men come to say this? There were a great many reasons why this was adopted. There are some shades of truth in the saying. It means different things in different mouths. Thus, with some, when it is said, "It matters little what a man's creed is, if his life is right," it is meant, "It matters little what a man's head-knowledge is so that he is sound in his heart." And sincerity here means not sincerity in belief, but sincerity in life, or godliness. And hence it expresses a great truth—a truth that is not enough recognized. There are two questions involved. One relates to what stands connected with the production of a godly disposition and a godly life; and the other relates to what, when a godly life and a godly disposition are produced, are their authority and their value.

Now if the question be one of education, of what is likely to make a man just and true, I say that it is of great importance what sort of truth you employ. For some kinds of teachings are a great deal more likely to produce godliness than others. But whatever the teaching has been, if there stands a man that is a good man, however strange it may be that such a creed should have such a disciple, however far he may be from the average results of the teaching of such things as he believes, his godliness is to be acknowledged in spite of the instrumentation, and you are to accept him as being a Christian man. If a man lives like a Christian, you are to admit that he is one, without regard to the church or faith to which he belongs.

Does success in life depend upon sincere believing or on right believing? Suppose a man should think that it made no difference what he believed, and should say to himself, "I want to raise some corn, but I have not the seed; so I will take some ashes and plant them; and I believe sincerely that they are as good as corn," would he have a crop of corn? What would his sincerity avail? The more sincere he was the worse it would be for him. If he was not sincere he might slip away and get a little corn, and plant that The more sincere he was, the more certainly he would not get a harvest. And in all material things, the more sincere you are, if you are right, the better; but the more sincere you are, if you are wrong, the worse. In the latter case sincerity is the mallet that drives home the mischief.

How is it in respect to commercial matters? A man says, "It makes no difference what I believe with regard to the conduct of my business, if I am only sincere." Does it not? Does it make no difference with the sale of a man's goods whether they are manufactured of one material or another? If a business man believes right in respect to his business, he prospers; and if he believes wrong, he does not prosper.

Take the navigator's business. A man says, "I have my own theories about astronomy, and I will sail my ship according to them. I do not believe the talk of the books on this subject. And it does not make much difference what a man believes respecting it." Does it make no difference what a man believes about charts? Suppose a man says, "I know the chart says that here are three fathoms of water, that here are two, and that here is one, but I do no believe it; I know that my ship draws sixteen feet of water, but I believe that I can run it over a twelve-feet bar" —does it make no difference what he believes? It makes the difference between shipwrecking and not shipwrecking!

And all through physical truth a man is bound to believe, not sincerely, but *correctly*. In all economic truths it is not enough for a man to believe sincerely: there he must believe accurately. In business, in manufacturing, in navigation, in all things that relate to the conduct of men in secular affairs, a man must believe that it is necessary for him to hold himself right—not merely sincere.

Take one thing further. There are affectional and social truths. Does it make no difference what a man believes in respect to these? A man says, "A truth of pride is the same as a truth of love, if a man is only sincere." Is there no difference between pride and vanity and selfishness, and tenderness and sympathy and love? And if a man has social intercourse, does it make no difference what view he takes of these things? Will it make no difference with his conduct if he thinks that pride and love are about the same thing, and that one is a proper substitute for the other? His sincerity makes the mischief worse in such a case.

It is only when we come to moral grounds that men begin to urge this declaration with any considerable degree of confidence. They reject it in its application to material truths, to physical sciences, to business, to social intercourse in life, and hold to the necessity of believing things as they are, and not simply sincerely. It is not until they come to religious truths that men begin to say, "It does not make much difference what a man believes."

Let us take the lower forms of moral truths, and see if it is so in our daily intercourse. You go to church and hear your minister preach about the necessity of believing such and such great doctrines, and on your way home you say, "It is not of so much importance what a man believes, if he is only sincere in it." When you get home you find that there is an altercation between the boy and the nurse. There is a lie between them somewhere. And the child falls on your theory, and says in respect to the wrongfulness of lying, "Father, I do not think it makes much difference what one believes, if he is only sincere." What do you think about this theory now?

You are bringing up your children. You can bring them up to believe in truth and honesty, or otherwise. Do you not desire to bring them up to believe that honesty is the best policy? Do you not desire to bring them up to believe that purity stands connected with their prosperity in after life? Do you not feel the greatest solicitude about the teaching of their minds? Are you not determined that they shall be brought up to distinguish the difference between truth and lies?

Let us apply the foregoing reasonings and explanations to the more important truths which we are set to preach. We are set to preach that this life is a very transient scene; that we are strangers and pilgrims here; that we are started here to be transplanted; that we are undergoing a process of education in this life, with reference to a life to come. The prime truth which we are set to preach is the transientness of the life that now is, and the *permanence* of the future life. And it is of supreme importance what a man believes in regard to that truth. If a man says, either practically or theoretically, "My existence in this world is all my life;" if he ignores the other life, and says, "I shall live just as long as I live here, and no longer," his character and conduct will

## THE TRUTH OF THE BIBLE PROVED. 73

be very different from what they would be if he believed in a life beyond the grave. A man that has no belief in the future will study how to extract the most happiness from this life. He never can have inspirations and heroisms who believes that his life will not extend beyond sixty or seventy years, like those which he experiences who believes that he shall live as long as God Almighty lives—for ever and for ever.

In this life men commonly live imperfect and sinful lives, and do much that is wrong, by voluntary transgression, as well as from the infirmities which come from crudeness and ignorance, where they should choose good or evil, right or wrong. Does it make no difference whether a man believes he is sinful or not? If a man is sick, does it make no difference whether he knows it or not? If a man has a disease working in his system, does it make no difference whether he understands it, and acts accordingly, or not? If a man's soul is diseased, does it make no difference whether he believes it or not?

We are taught in the Word of God that all men are sin-struck, and that every man that lives needs the grace and forbearance and forgiveness of God, and moral renovation at the hands of God. If a man believes that he is good enough, of course he becomes listless and heedless and inattentive. If another man by his side believes that he is sinful, and needs to be born again, with what a constantly quickened and watchful conscience must he needs live! and how, with all his moral power, must he perpetually strive to live a godly life. Some men believe that though we ought to become good, goodness is exclusively the creature of our own volition; that all men have a spark of goodness in them, and have but to kindle that to a flame in order to be pervaded with goodness; that we are all good in a small measure, and that to become very good we have only to cultivate the goodness we have. But the Scripture teaches us that we must have the beginning of our spiritual life founded in the power of God; and that the beginnings of a Christian life must come by communication of our heart with the heart of God. Here are two radically opposite views. Does it make no difference which a man takes? One leads to morality of a lower kind, and the other to religious emotions and a religious life. They diverge and go in opposite directions. It is not my business to show which is best, but to show that one goes one way and the other another.

Does it make no difference what a man believes in respect to the character of God, the nature of the divine government in this world, its claims upon us, and our obligations under it? If a man believes that God sits above indifferent to the affairs of this life, and too quiescent to attend to the little disturbances of sin, and that he overlooks transgression, that man must inevitably come to a state of moral indifference. But if a man believes that God cannot look upon sin with allowance, that he abhors iniquity, and that unless we turn from our wicked ways he will lay his hand on the sword, and set himself forth as the maintainer of law, and justice, and integrity, that man cannot help being morally solicitous. Does it make no difference what a man believes on these subjects?

Go into New York, and in the Sixth Ward you shall find two representative men. One says, I voted for the judge, and helped put him where he is, and he will wink at my crimes. I can drink as much as I please on Sundays and on week-days, and he will not disturb me. He is easy and good-natured, and he is not going to be hard with me if I do break the laws a little." And the man, because he believes that the judge does not care for his wickedness, and will not punish him, grows bold and corrupt in transgression. But at length he is arraigned, he is brought before the court, and he finds there instead of his bribed judge, a white-faced man—not red-faced; one of those men with a long head upward—not backward and downward; a man with no rolling or rocking of the eye at all; a man with a full value of justice and truth. The culprit begins to make shuffling excuses. The judge listens to none of them, and reads the law, and says, " Your conduct is herein condemned," and sends him away to receive his just deserts. When the man has expiated his crime, he goes around in the same ward, and says, "You must walk straight hereafter. The judge that sits on the bench now is not the jolly old judge that used to sit there. If you go before him he will make you smart." Does it not make a difference what a man believes about a judge? If he believes that he is a lenient, conniving judge, does it not make him careless? and if he believes that he is a straightforward, just judge, does it not make him afraid of transgression ?

Now lift up the judge's bench, and make it the judgment-seat; and take out the human judge, and put God Almighty there. If men believe him to be an all-smiling God; a God that is all sunshine; an all-sympathizing God; a God that is nothing but kindness and goodness and gentleness, they say to themselves, "We will do as we have a mind to." Take away that miserable slander upon the revealed character of God, and lift up the august front of Justice, on whose brow love proudly sits, and let men see that there is a vast Heart of love and gentleness, indeed, but that will by no means clear the guilty, and they will take more heed to their conduct. Does it, then, make no difference what a man believes about God's nature, and his manner of dealing with men? It makes all the difference between laxity and earnestness; between an endeavor to live truly and no endeavor at all in that direction; between right and wrong conduct.

What, then, is the application, finally, of this? Why, it is just this: that it makes all the difference in the world what you believe in respect to these truths that stand connected with godliness; that stand connected with purity of thought, purity of motive, purity of disposition.

On such questions as pertain to true piety, to right and wrong, the Holy Scriptures are very explicit. "For there is a way which seemeth right to a man; but the end thereof are the ways of death." Before the apostle Paul's conversion, he says, "I verily thought with myself that I ought to do many things contrary to the name of Jesus of Nazareth." In this he was sincere, but mistaken. Therefore in reference to right living, you need the Bible for your constant guide. It is God's medicine book. You are sick. You are mortally struck through with disease. There is no human remedy for your trouble. But here is God's medicine book. If you read it for life, for health, for growth in righteousness, then blessed is your reading of it; but if you read it for disputation and dialectical ingenuities, it is no more to you than Bacon's "Novum Organum" would be.

It is the book of life; it is the book of everlasting life; so take heed how you read it. In reading it see that you have the truth, and not the mere semblance of it. You cannot live without it. You die forever unless you have it to teach you what are your relations to God and eternity. May God guide you away from all cunning appearances of truth set to deceive men, and make you love the truth. Above all other things may God make you honest in interpreting it and applying it to your daily life and disposition.

# (2.) GOD AND HIS MORAL GOVERNMENT.

## CHAPTER XII.

### A SUPREME MORAL GOVERNOR INDISPENSABLE.

Without a supreme Almighty Governor, controlling the planetary worlds by providential laws, there would be continuous confusion among them. And, in order that the human family may be restrained and regulated in their relations to their Maker and each other, in a moral point of view, He must exert not only a providential but a moral government over them, with just and absolute laws and retributive penalties, and effective motives adapted to promote obedience to these laws, by appealing to their love, their sense of gratitude, and their fears. And in the state or nation there must be a supreme human governor, to whom strict obedience should be rendered by the people. "Let every soul be subject to the higher powers, for there is no power but of God." And in the family the husband and father must be the head and governor, in order to secure peace and prosperity among its members. "The head of every man is Christ, and the head of the woman is the man." "Wives, submit yourselves unto your own husbands, as unto the Lord." "Servants, be obedient to them that are your masters according to the flesh, as unto Christ."

And from experience and observation we know that where there is no recognized head and governor to enforce law and authority, there must be continual discord, fretfulness, and confusion in the family. And with such facts before us, we are convinced that all free moral agents, capable of knowing right from wrong, need a supreme moral governor to regulate all their moral conduct by moral laws, enforced with rewards and penalties.

As Dr. Hawes observes: "The moral government of God is a government of law and motive, administered over men through the instrumentality of rewards and punishments, to be awarded to them according to their respective characters. Take away, now, the doctrine of a future state of retribution, and what, I ask, becomes of the moral government of God? It is deprived of all its power to influence the heart and life, because deprived of all the motives by which it secures obedience and deters from crime. Its laws cease to be laws, and become mere counsel or advice, with no sanctions to enforce their claims, and no means to act on men as voluntary and accountable agents. Let not the stale sophism be repeated that men are rewarded and punished in this life according to their deserts. If anything can prove moral insanity, it is a belief that God now dispenses rewards and punishments to men according to their respective characters. Nothing can be plainer, than that neither 'love nor hatred can be known' by the condition of men in this world. Deny then that there is a future state, in which the righteous are to be rewarded and the wicked punished, and you sweep away every vestige of a righteous moral government over the children of men. The whole world becomes a vast scene of disorder and confusion, 'where mankind may live as they list and fare as they can, having nothing to dread, and nothing to hope for hereafter, on account of anything they do, or neglect to do, in this life.' For what remains, I ask, to engage obedience or prevent transgression, when the *sanctions* of the divine government are gone? Do you say gratitude and love—the pleasure of doing right and the remorse of doing wrong? Try the experiment in regard to human governments. Let it be proclaimed throughout the community, and among all classes of rogues and villains, that there are no courts of justice, no prisons, no places or instruments of justice; what, suppose you, would be the effect? Would the pleasure of doing right engage obedience to the laws, or secure the peace and good order of society? Would the inconveniences of remorse prevent swindling and theft, robbery and murder, and convert all the outcasts of society into honest and good men? Why then talk of gratitude and love, of the present pleasures of virtue and sufferings of vice, as sufficient to secure obedience under the divine government? If a system of human legislation without rewards and punishments would be altogether inefficacious and nugatory, why would not the same be true of the divine government?

"Whatever view I take of the subject, to me it seems too plain to admit of denial, that Universalism destroys the divine moral government, and takes from God a character, in the belief of which we can alone approach him acceptably; that of his being a 're-warder of them that diligently seek him.' *Heb.* xi: 6.

"It of course denies the present to be a state of probation. Such a state implies that men are now on trial for eternity; that they are acting under the government of God, with reference to a future retribution; and that there is an inseparable connection between their conduct in this life and their condition in the life to come."

# CHAPTER XIII.

## THE PERFECT GOODNESS AND SEVERITY OF GOD IN GOVERNMENT.

The goodness of God comprises in an infinite degree every amiable and moral quality. "God is love." He is impartially benevolent. He is disposed to communicate to his creatures the greatest amount of happiness of which their moral characters are susceptible. He is disposed to bestow upon them every blessing which is proper and best for them, and which is consistent for Him in view of His own glory and the highest good of the universe, to bestow for time and eternity.

God's goodness is manifest in Creation, Providence and Redemption. The fact that God has so adapted the external world and our intellectual, moral and physical constitutions as to make us happy, proves his benevolence toward us. As God's will, expressed in his moral law, requires us to be universally and perfectly benevolent, he must be perfectly benevolent himself.

As God's will awards eternal happiness to the benevolent, and eternal misery to the malevolent, he must also be infinitely and perfectly benevolent himself.

But it may be objected that our sufferings here are inconsistent with God's perfect benevolence. I reply, pain is only incidental to the attainment of a benevolent end. Teeth were not made to ache—pain is only incidental to their existence and abuse. All suffering is the result of infraction of laws established for the accomplishment of benevolent ends. It may also be objected that the existence of sin, and its penalty, is inconsistent with God's perfect benevolence. I reply, our non-existence would be a greater negative evil, depriving the human family of the happiness which so greatly exceeds the misery in the present world. And as we hope that the number finally saved (reckoning all young infants and the greatly surpassing millions of Christians who will live in the millenium age) over those who have previously died in impenitence, will make it better on the whole for the race to have existed than not to have existed.

Furthermore, it seems probable as all free agents are liable to sin, that God cannot wisely prevent all sin in the best system of moral government. It may be impracticable to construct and regulate the best physical, intellectual and moral universe, in any way so as to avoid all friction. Our most profound divines think that this world seems to have been designed for the happiness of virtuous beings, and in accomplishing this, disciplinary chastisements to sinners are incidental and absolutely necessary. As the most skillful machinist is unable to avoid all friction in machinery, though he should possess many million of times his present power and skill, it may not be within the province of Almighty power and infinite wisdom, so to construct and create a system, inhabited by free moral and responsible agents, so as to avoid all liability to the commission of sin, which inevitably ensures suffering at some period of physical and moral existence.

The divine method of government is not arbitrary, unreasonable, or needlessly severe, and therefore it is absolutely just, and the most perfect government for controlling men. Hence it should be the model of all human governments. In God's moral government, goodness and forbearance are exercised to their utmost limits. But when kindness and persuasion have been employed to their utmost, and have failed to preserve obedience and uprightness, or to restrain and reclaim the stubborn and persistent offender from the violation of law, God applies the severest and most frightful penalties.

"Behold, therefore, the goodness and severity of God; on them which fell, severity; but toward thee, goodness; otherwise thou shalt be cut off."

And this kind of government which encourages virtue by rewards, and restrains sin by fearful penalties, is the most effective, whether divine or human, for maintaining authority and in securing the most perfect obedience.

Is there not some danger, in the present day, of God's love being presented to sinners to the exclusion altogether of his justice? The late F. W. Robertson speaks well on this subject: "Here is an eternal truth with which we would not part: God must hate sin, and be forever sin's enemy. Because He is the Lord of love, therefore must he be a consuming fire to evil. God is against evil, but for us. If, then, we sin, He must be against us. In sinning, we identify ourselves with evil, therefore we must endure the consuming fire. O brethren, in this soft age in which we live, it is good to fall back on the first principles of everlasting truth. We have come to think that education may be maintained by mere laws of love, instead of discipline, and that public punishment may be abolished. We say that these things are contrary to the gospel; and here, doubtless, there is an underlying truth. It is true that there may be a severity in education which defeats itself; it is true that love and tenderness may do more than severity—but yet under a system of mere love and tenderness, no character can acquire manliness or firmness. When you have once got rid of the idea of public punishment, then by degrees you will also get rid of the idea of sin. Where is it written in the word of God that the sword of his minister is to be borne in vain ? In this world of groaning and of anguish, tell us where it is that the law which links suffering to sin has ceased to act? Nay, so long as there is evil, so long will there be penalty, and woe to that man who attempts to contradict the eternal system of God. So long as the spirit of evil ir in the world, so long must human punishment remain to bear its testimony that the God of the universe is a righteous God."

## CHAPTER XIV.

### ERRONEOUS VIEWS OF GOD CORRECTED.

In the palmy days and innocency of our first parents, the woman said unto the serpent, "We may eat of the fruit of the trees of the garden. But of the tree which is in the midst of the garden, God hath said, 'Ye shall not eat of it, neither shall ye touch it, lest ye die.'" And the serpent said unto the woman, "Ye shall not surely die." But they yielded to the temptation of the adversary, by sinning against God, and brought ruin upon all their descendents.

They, while in a state of innocency, were overcome by temptation; but their descendents ever since, being in a state of apostacy, have yielded more easily to the temptation of false reasoning, in reference to the character of God and His government, and the threatened penalty of His violated laws upon all impenitent sinners. And from erroneous premises some of their posterity falsely reason that the paternal and compassionate character of the Almighty is such that He can never execute upon the most persistent and rebellious of any of the children of His own creation the penalty of " eternal punishment," as He threatens so repeatedly in His most Holy Word. But in reference to all such fallacious reasoners God says, " Thou thoughtest that I was altogether such a one as thyself; but I will reprove thee and set them in order before thine eyes."

And it is, it seems to me, just here that the fundamental error and false method of reasoning concerning the moral character of God commences, on the part of those who deny the eternal punishment of the impenitent dead. They falsely maintain that the Almighty and Just Governor of mankind will be controlled like themselves by human sympathy toward the incorrigibly wicked, rather than by absolute justice.

Under these new circumstances, with the increased power of the great tempter, false and heretical teachers have arisen, who maintain " that all we can know of the divine nature must be learned by reasoning from those elements and qualities which are found in the human constitution." They maintain that man was made in the divine image, with certain qualities, that by his moral consciousness he might have a true and vital conception of his Heavenly Father.

Now if this be a correct method of reasoning, from human nature in a state of moral uprightness, must it not be a dangerous and absurd fallacy when applied to the same nature in a state of apostacy and rebellion? By reasoning from man's disordered finite moral powers, to the perfect and infinite moral nature of Jehovah, does it not lead us "to think of men above that which is written" more highly than we ought to think? Does it not encourage the fundamental errors of "false teachers, who bring in damnable heresies, even denying the Lord that bought them, and bringing upon themselves swift destruction?"

Is it not a false method of reasoning from our constitutional dread of suffering, and from our natural compassion, as well as our very low estimate of the evil of sin and its dreadful consequences, that God will not render to every man according to his deeds in "the day of wrath and revelation of the righteous judgment of God?"

Is it not more rational and logical to learn God's true character and government as He manifests Himself in His providence and from the definite teachings of his infallible word? All that the goodness of God's character demands is that He govern in such a manner as will secure the greatest practicable amount of good in the universe. That great temporal sufferings are consistent with this, is proved by facts; and who but God is competent to decide that the eternal sufferings of those who die in sin and impenitence are not consistent? His character demands that He should restrain the greatest possible number from sinning by threatening the most dreadful penalty.

Therefore are the impenitent dead "set for an example, suffering the vengeance of eternal fire." It is very plain to every real Christian (if not to unbelievers) that God has clearly revealed Himself, in nature and revelation, as a Being of perfect goodness, justice, mercy and truth. And those who believe in or worship an imaginary being with different attributes, are "vain in their imaginations, and their foolish heart is darkened; and change the glory of the incorruptible God into an image made like to corruptible man;" and are doomed to fearful disappointments in the judgment day.

"The Lord is long suffering, and of great mercy, forgiving iniquity and transgression, and by no means clearing the guilty." "It is a fearful thing to fall into the hands of the living God." "Except ye repent, ye shall all likewise perish." "What wilt thou say when He shall punish thee?"

# CHAPTER XV.

MYSTERY OF MYSTERIES. SIN AND SUFFERING.

It seems difficult if not impossible for us to perceive how to reconcile the perfect goodness, wisdom and power of the Almighty, with His sufferance of sin, contention and misery, in our world, and in the endless punishment of impenitent sinners beyond the present life. But nature and revelation teach us that these are facts in the Divine character, and in the administration of His providential and moral government. Hence we must conclude that God in His infinite knowledge perceives that there is harmony and consistency between these facts, which appear to our finite minds unreasonable and irreconcilable. Of course with our very limited powers, we do not and cannot know that omniscience and omnipotence could wisely create and constitute a system of moral government, with free, intelligent, moral agents, who should not be liable to sin, and suffer both here and hereafter.

Hence we may wisely conclude that what God does, He knows to be on the whole, the wisest and best, and it becomes us to be both submissive and trustful, for he can be neither arbitrary, unreasonable or malevolent.

As Prof. Wright observes, "The greatest of all mysteries is that God has thus endowed man with free-will, and has allowed him to sin; yet the facts cannot be disputed. God has created man in his own image, and suffered him to deface it. God has made for himself a temple in the human heart, and suffered it to be defiled. The reason cannot solve the parodox of an Almighty and Benevolent Being hating sin, and yet not preventing it. The essential mystery shrouding this question does not pertain to the endless continuance of punishment or sin, but to the permission of sin at all, and of the evils we know to follow in its train. The monotonous list of crimes that is served up to us at each breakfast by the daily papers, should restrain us from speculating too freely upon the Creator's power to eliminate sin from the system He has established. Perhaps the *elimination of sin* would involve the *elimination of the system.* Now that the creation exists, it is our province to study the conditions of its existence, and to adjust ourselves to them. In speculating with reference to what the Creator will do, we are not at liberty to close our eyes to what He has done. What we know is the only proper basis from which to reason with reference to what we do not know. From the existence of sin we know that there is some inherent difficulty in the way of securing the universal reign of righteousness among beings possessed of such powers as the Creator has bestowed upon the human race. The wisdom of God appears in the creation as well as in the government of His creatures. The wisdom displayed in the Creator's plan of government cannot run counter to that displayed in the creation. God has seen fit to make us so that we can defy His authority. God has seen fit to create the world so that as a result of sin there is an untold amount of misery in it. When any one can reconcile the present state of things in this world with his ideas of divine goodness, and wisdom, and power, we will listen to his speculative arguments against endless punishment."

# CHAPTER XVI.

## WHY DO THE BEST OF CHRISTIANS SOMETIMES SUFFER IN THIS LIFE MORE THAN THE WORST OF SINNERS?

"The goodness of God endureth continually." "O that men would praise the Lord for His goodness, and for His wonderful words to the children of men." "For our light affliction, which is but for a moment, worketh for us a far more exceeding and eternal weight of glory." From this declaration concerning affliction, Christians will doubtless be much happier in heaven for their innocent sufferings on earth. From this inspired statement concerning affliction, it seems probable that the best of Christians, who sometimes suffer more here than the grossly wicked, may experience greater happiness in heaven in proportion to their sufferings in this life.

It is plainly the teachings of Scripture that the ordinary afflictions of life, when rightly improved, are a means of sanctification, promoting our present and future blessedness. " Earthly sufferings increase our heavenly glory." "The affliction," as one has said, "is in order to the glory." It has (as sanctification) a positive and most important agency in preparing believers for their future triumph.

"Whom the Lord loveth He chasteneth," and the troubles of this life are the crucible in which He purges His people of their dross and refines their graces."

"Our trials come in mercy. The painful mysteries of our lot, our losses, our distresses, our conflicts, are the assayers fine, designed and adapted to consume the dross and refine the gold. He afflicts not willingly, but because He is a Father; and, as a Father, whom He chastens He will gloriously reward."

And, still further, may we not rationally and hopefully consider it probable that in the future world it will be found that the greatest sufferings of those who were most perfectly sanctified here will be rewarded with an increased weight of glory? Will not those who were the most holy in this life, who have been the greatest sufferers here, be in some measure and proportion rewarded with a higher state of blessedness in heaven? Will not the inexplicable mystery of their greatest sufferings here be in a measure solved by the compensation of more glorious rewards hereafter? May not such afflictions especially "work for us a far more exceeding and eternal weight of glory?"

> "For God has marked each sorrowing day,
> And numbered every secret tear.
> And Heaven's long age of bliss shall pay,
> For all His children suffer here."

In Heaven, "every man shall receive his own reward, according to his own labor." His reward shall be in proportion to his faithfulness in his Master's service. He shall "receive the things done in his body, according to that he hath done." And if the best and most faithful workers in the vineyard of the Lord, in the world of glory, shall be rewarded with increased felicity and blessedness in proportion to their faithful services in this world shall not the most purely sanctified of God's deeply afflicted children, who suffer most here, be compensated with an increased and "far more exceeding and eternal weight of glory" hereafter?

If the devoted missionary of the cross, in Christian or in heathen land, who has "turned many to righteousness" shall have a proportionate number of stars in his crown of rejoicing in that day when God shall make up His jewels, shall not the sanctified Christian who has spent the greater portion of a long life "in the furnace of affliction, seven times heated," with such patient and submissive fortitude as to adorn religion with increased lustre, and has done more good, and thus impressed the world with its imperishable value and importance, be compensated with an increased degree of imperishable glory in heaven?

When we contemplate the unfathomable mysteries of sin and suffering, which prevail in our world and baffle our sagacity, we must modestly refer the difficulties by which we are embarrassed, to our own ignorance, and find consolation and satisfaction in the thought that there must be principles or facts yet undiscovered by finite minds, which if understood and comprehended would perfectly explain them and render them reasonable and consistent. We should now endeavor to realize that these infinitesimal facts are only parts of a stupendous whole. We must rest assured that although " clouds and darkness are round about Him, righteousness and judgment are the habitation of His throne."

# (3.) RETRIBUTION.

## CHAPTER XVII.

### PROBATION LIMITED TO THE PRESENT LIFE.

The Bible plainly teaches that the present life is man's only period for preparing for his eternal home, and the future life is the place for his permanent and endless retribution. Its language is explicit, and fearfully emphatic. "Prepare to meet thy God. Be ye also ready. Flee from the wrath to come. The time is short. Whatsoever thy hand findeth to do, do it with thy might; for there is no work, nor device, nor knowledge, nor wisdom, in the grave whither thou goest." Yet with all such alarming admonitions, men now dead in trespasses and sin, while the Scriptures reason of righteousness, temperance, and judgment to come, like trembling Felix, answer: "Go thy way for this time, when I have a convenient season I will call for thee." But God says, "It is appointed unto men once to die, but after this the judgment."

"For we must all appear before the judgment seat of Christ, that every one may receive the things done in his body, according to that he hath done, whether it be good or bad."

And in addition to such teachings as these, it is plainly taught that there is permanence of character for all the dead. "He that is unjust, let him be unjust still; and he that is filthy, let him be filthy still; and he that is righteous, let him be righteous still; and he that is holy, let him be holy still."

If the Bible were merely silent on the point of probation beyond the grave, it would be equivalent to the denial of such a state, for the love of men for sinful gratification now, induces them to defer repentance and reformation as long as they dare. And certainly, if they could reasonably hope for another trial after death, they would be greatly relieved from the present solicitude in reference to their future condition. And if the truth in the matter could relieve their fearful anxiety, in reference to their future state, would not God dissipate their needless solicitude, by disclosing the fact of a future probation? But by examining His word we find not the slightest intimation that those who die in impenitency and unbelief, will ever turn from sin to holiness.

The Scriptures are indeed very explicit, in warning men now to flee from the wrath to come; but they shed not a solitary ray of light on the way of escape from sin and misery in the future world. They do not intimate that there is any such thing as passing from hell to heaven.

In the parable of the wise and foolish virgins, who

represent the condition of the righteous and the wicked in the future world, we find that the former being in readiness for the feast were admitted, and the latter were forever excluded. " The bridegroom came; and they that were ready went in with him to the marriage, and the door was shut. Afterwards came also the other virgins, saying Lord, Lord, open to us. But he answered and said, verily I say unto you, I know you not. Watch therefore; for ye know neither the day nor the hour wherein the Son of Man cometh."

As we know not when our Lord shall call us away from this life, we must be constantly prepared so that we may then be admitted to heaven, for those who are then unprepared can never be admitted.

In the parable of the barren fig tree, we are taught that this life is a season of probationary discipline; but there is no indication of any future trial period. After the tree had been sufficiently tried, the owner of the vineyard directed the dresser to cut it down. "Why cumbereth it the ground?" And certainly after it is cut down, it cannot be tried again. And the sinner who is cut off from this life will not have another probationary trial.

If men were to have a future probation, they might wisely give their whole attention now to the things of this life, and attend to religion after death. But the Scriptures discountenance entirely such a course. Their language is directly the reverse. "Seek ye first the kingdom of God and His righteousness." Make religion your present business. "To-day, if ye will hear His voice, harden not your hearts." It is folly to seek the world now, with the hope of an opportunity to prepare for heaven hereafter. "For what shall it profit a man if he shall gain the whole world and lose his own soul." He must seek his salvation now, or fail forever. For Jesus has said, "I go my way, and ye shall seek me, and shall die in your sins; whither I go ye cannot come." And in His commission to His disciples He gives no intimation that men can prepare for heaven after death. "Go ye into all the world and preach the gospel to every creature. He that believeth, and is baptized, shall be saved; but he that believeth not shall be damned." Sinners must believe now, and be saved, or never enter heaven.

# CHAPTER XVIII.

NO SECOND PROBATION IN THE INTERMEDIATE STATE, OR DURING THE SLEEP OF THE BODIES OF THE DEAD.

Here let us inquire what is to be the condition of the soul between death and the judgment. Is this intermediate state one in which the offers of mercy through Christ, so freely extended here, are continued? May we hope that some who are incorrigible in their wickedness this side the grave, will repent in that interval which occurs between death and the judgment?

It is commonly believed by second probationists that there will be no second probation for deliberate and continued rejectors of the gospel here. But those who have not had the motives of the gospel presented to them during life, such as young children, feeble-minded idiots, and many of the heathen, will have them presented to them, and have the opportunity of repentance and salvation, before the final judgment. This is the form of the heretical question, now greatly exciting public attention and discussion.

But what is meant by the separate or intermediate state? The state in which the soul has a conscious existence between the death and resurrection of the body. But where is the soul after separation from the body at death, previous to the resurrection and the general judgment? Does it go immediately at death to its eternal destination? From the aspirations of the apostle Paul it would seem that he expected nothing short of perfect happiness immediately upon leaving the world. We are confident, I say, and willing, rather to be absent from the body, and be present with the Lord. I am in a straight betwixt two, having a desire to depart and be with Christ which is far better. Hence, we conclude that all true Christians immediately at death enter into more intimate communion with Christ, and they wait for the glorious resurrection of the body, and for the consummation of the kingdom of God. For our Saviour said to the penitent thief on the cross, "To-day shalt thou be with me in paradise."

But what will become of the wicked, immediately after death? "The wicked is driven away in his wickedness, but the righteous hath hope in his death." "The wicked shall be turned into hell, and all the nations that forget God." Hence we conclude that all mankind will exist in the life to come, in a conscious active and happy, or unhappy, state, as they shall be holy or unholy when they depart the present life. They pass immediately into this condition of existence at death. "The soul will immediately pass into a state of happiness, or misery, and the body shall dissolve to dust, whence it was taken."

The soul does not become lifeless with the body, nor does it sleep or lie dormant after the death of the body, till the general resurrection; but it is sensible and active. For "it came to pass that the beggar died, and was carried by angels into Abraham's bosom; the rich man also died, and was buried; and in hell he lifted up his eyes, being in torment, and seeth Abraham afar off, and Lazarus in his bosom. But Abraham said, 'Son, remember that thou in thy lifetime received the good things, and likewise Lazarus evil things; but now he is comforted and thou art tormented.'"

But in all these inspired instructions concerning death and the intermediate state, there is not the faintest reference to any classes of persons, who are in a state of second probation. But we do read, "He that is unrighteous, let him do unrighteousness still; and he that is filthy, let him be made filthy still; and he that is righteous, let him do righteousness still; and he that is holy, let him be made holy still. Behold, I come quickly; and my reward is with me, to render to each man according as his work is."

But it may be asked where are the myriads of young children, who die before they attain a period or age of responsibility? "The disciples came to Jesus saying, 'Who is the greatest in the kingdom of heaven?' And Jesus called a little child unto Him, and set him in the midst of them, and said: 'Verily, I say unto you, except ye be converted, and become as little children, ye shall not enter into the kingdom of heaven.' Whosoever, therefore, shall humble himself as this little child, the same is greatest in the kingdom of heaven." And may not enfeebled idiots, who have no more development or responsibility than young children, be reckoned in the same category in the future world? For "to whomsoever much is given, of him shall much be required." And of course to whom little is given, little will be required.

(EXTRACT.—MEN IGNORANT OF THE GOSPEL.)

But is it reasonable to punish men who have never heard of the gospel? They are punished not for distinctively rejecting the gospel, but for distinctively rejecting the law. God has given His law to them as really as to us. He has threatened them with its penalty as really as He has threatened us. They "are without excuse," for on their consciences, as on tables of living stone, God has inscribed His commandment. Of the written law, the objector says: "As many as have sinned without law, will have a probation after death." Of the same law the apostle says: "As many as have sinned without law, shall also perish without law."—Romans i: 12-16. Our compassionate Redeemer has taught us that if we, with our larger knowledge, disobey His commands, we shall be punished with many stripes, and if other men, with their smaller knowledge disobey these commands, they will be punished with few stripes. *But they will be punished.* If they do not deserve to be punished, then they have not sinned. If they have sinned then they deserve to be punished. If they have committed ten degrees of wrong, they will endure ten degrees of remorse. If they have committed only one degree of wrong, they will endure only one degree of remorse. But, ten degrees or one degree of remorse, it cannot be avoided unless the wrong be forgiven. According to the mere constitution of the soul, it can never end unless conscience loses its normal power.

It were singular, indeed, if men were to be freed from penal remorse on account of their ignorance, when their ignorance implies the sin; when having eyes they see not, because they will not see; when knowing certain parts of the truth, they hold back other parts of it, because they choose not to think of it! It were singular, indeed, if the heathen were to be freed from penal remorse because Christians have disobeyed their Lord's command to go into all the world and preach the gospel to every creature! Singular, if the refusal of Christians to evangelize the world should be turned into a bounty upon the heathen, and release them from the claims of the law as it is written on the most authoritative part of their constitution.

But it is said that our Lord, immediately after His resurrection, preached to the spirits in prison; and by implication it may be said that sinners may be preached to after death. I reply that there is no clear evidence that Christ ever preached to sinners in the future state. And we have never yet learned that any have been converted after death by the preaching of our Lord. But for the sake of the argument, let us admit that while Christ's body was resting in Joseph's new tomb, his soul went to some place where were confined in prison certain departed spirits, who aforetime were disobedient in the days of Noah, and preached to them. If our Lord did preach to the spirits in prison after death, He obviously preached to them the same gospel He did on earth. He then told sinners if they should be cast in prison, they should not come out thence till they had paid the utmost farthing. If He went down to hell to preach to the lost spirits there, He doubtless told them, 'You must remain here until you have suffered all that your sins deserve.' What influence then would His preaching have toward releasing them from the place of torment? It must still remain true: (1) that there is no evidence that He preached to any other departed spirits than the comparatively few herein specified; (2) that it is inexplicable why those few should have been singled out for such a mission, who were certainly among the most wicked of men, and would appear to have had, through Noah and his influence, a much fairer "chance" than millions of others, presumably then in Hades, who had lived and died in an altogether unillumined darkness of paganism; (3) that there is no evidence that Christ's preaching to these people on this occasion did them any good; (4) that there is no probability that such preaching ever was, or can be repeated; but many circumstances to imply that, as the incidents of this obscure scene can never recur, so this account of them can reasonably afford neither proof, precedent nor even trusty remote suggestion of any purpose of God, or any law of His government by which probation after death becomes a likelihood for any who leave this world in impenitence.

# CHAPTER XIX.

### CHRIST AND ETERNAL PUNISHMENT.

(EXTRACT.)

A sincere inquirer for truth, however he may be perplexed by the doctrine of eternal punishment, is compelled to accept it, because it is so plainly taught and so often urged by the Saviour himself.

Christ, in these declarations of eternal punishment, never betrays one symptom of doubt or delicacy, as if there might be some injustice or over-severity in them, such as needs to be carefully qualified. He plainly enough has no such struggles of mind on the subject as we have. His most delicate, tenderly-sensitive humanity gives no single token of being either offended or tried by the fact of so great severities. It cannot be that He is untroubled by questions on this subject because He is less tender of man's lot or of God's honor than we are, or because He is not far enough on in the world's progress to have had our great theologic problems occur to Him.

Perhaps we shall not be able to solve this strangely

unquestioning manner of His, but I strongly suspect that the secret of it lies in the fact that He has a way of conceiving the matter and manner of eternal punishment, such as leaves our modern questions out of sight and does not even allow them to occur. Perhaps He only thinks of the bad man going on to eternity in his badness, and the laws of retribution as going along with him to keep his voluntary bad deeds company, much as they do here; regarding the malefactor as a malefactor still, and suffering, at any given moment, for being just what he is at that moment—that, and nothing more. God has, in fact, put nothing of his pain upon him; he only takes it on himself; and there is really no more reason to be troubled about the severity of his lot, than there is here, in the retributions of this life.

He uses, it must be admitted, the most appalling figures—"outer darkness," "great gulf fixed," "thirst," "torment," "wailing," "weeping," "a worm that dieth not," "a fire that is not quenched,"—but He has no misgiving; probably because words of any kind are so impotent in giving the due impression of any state unrealized, and need to be even violently overdrawn to answer their object. However this may be, it is quite evident that the tough questions of our modern philanthropism have either not arrived, or are quite gone by, and that, notwithstanding His intense love for mankind, His feeling still goes with the primitive order of God's retribution, adding even heavier emphasis from His own personal indignations.

What was the attitude of Jesus Christ toward the questions of possible future probation after death,

# RETRIBUTION.

and of remediless and everlasting torment of all those in every time and place, who die impenitent?

In answer, I beg leave to suggest, in their most condensed form, the following considerations, viz:

First. At His advent Christ found the great mass of the Jewish nation actual believers in the future eternal punishment of those who die in sin. This is made clear from the statement of Josephus. And there is no doubt that the Pharisees of the New Testament times believed in eternal damnation.

Second. Christ must have known that this faith on this subject was thus pre-existent in the minds of those whom He came to lead in the way of life; and must have realized that for Him to say nothing in contradiction thereof would be to seal to their convictions its truth by the large consent of His silence. Yea, further, that for Him to refer to that subject in any historic or casual way without condemning such faith, would be to give it still more confirmation of His manifested consideration issuing in the natural seeming of approval. Such being the facts, it becomes necessary further to decide that whenever He uttered Himself upon the circle of related truths, His language must necessarily take on the force of the fullest endorsement of the doctrine substantially as the Jews held it, unless it were distinctly in opposition thereto; because, under the circumstances, His intent must be presumed to have been to indorse, unless He did in terms oppose.

Third. Now, as a matter of fact, Christ is never recorded to have uttered one word of remonstrance with the Jews for their belief in the future eternal punishment of those who die in their sins. We cannot doubt that His solicitude for the glory of God must at least have equaled that of those who are in our day most anxious to relieve the divine character of what seems to them the deep dishonor involved in the ancient doctrine under discussion; yet He undertook no explanation; least of all did He anywhere say or hint, "Ye do greatly err in supposing that My Father can do such things."

Fourth. Christ never said anything which, when fairly interpreted by its obvious connection and clear intent, even seems to look in the direction of denying the opinion on this subject then commonly received in Palestine. At least I have searched for such utterances from His lips in vain. And, on this point, I ask leave to fortify myself by the avowal of that venerable, industrious and illustrious exegete, Professor Stuart, who says:

"Why have those holy teachers, Christ and His apostles, failed to make *explicit* declarations, which admit of no doubt and no misinterpretation in regard to this matter? If I should be told, as I may be by some, that they have made such declarations, my answer is, that after making the Scriptures the principal object of my study through most of my life, I have not been able to find them. I have sought for them with great solicitude; in one sense I can say truly, that I have hoped to find them. . . . . I cannot find in the Scriptures a *disavowal* of the usual belief of the primitive age as to endless punishment; nor can I find where an opinion contrary to this is taught, or even suggested, in the Bible."

The Bible plainly teaches: (1) There is a sin which cannot be forgiven, so that all who are guilty of it must be hopelessly and forever lost. (2) Death concludes the opportunity of human penitence. (3) At the end of the world the wicked are to be punished, and the righteous rewarded. (4) The dead are to be raised—the good to life, the bad to condemnation. (5) There is to be a day of final reckoning, when the Son of Man will judge the world; whose awards will send the wicked away into punishment, and the righteous into life. (6) This future punishment of the wicked, equally with the future life of the righteous, will be without end.

The punishment of the impenitent dead must be endless, because the scriptural terms which allude to it denote absolute eternity.

Says Dr. N. Adams: " There is, we all admit, such a thing as forever. If the Bible speaks of the natural attributes of God, His eternity is of course brought to view, and there must be a term, or terms, to convey the idea. Now it is apparent to all, that the words eternal, everlasting, forever, never of themselves signify a limited duration. No one ever learns from these words that the duration to which they refer is less than infinite. The idea of limitation, if it be obtained, is always derived from the context. It is, moreover, true beyond the possibility of dispute, that the words eternal, everlasting and forever, always mean the whole of something. There is no instance in which they are used to denote a part of a things duration. It is always the entire period for which that thing is to last. This, no one will call in question. It is well understood that the words forever and everlasting are used to express a duration commensurate with the nature of the thing spoken of. Everlasting mountains are coeval with creation, and are to endure as long as the earth. A servant forever, is a servant for life. We cannot take the sense which the word has in connection with a certain thing, and by it prove or disprove anything relating to a totally different thing. We cannot prove, for example, that mountains will not last to the end of time, because forever applied to a servant means only for life. We must consider the nature of the object to which the word is applied. When it is applied to the Most High, of course it means unlimited duration. Now the words which convey the idea of absolute eternity, are applied for example to mountains, to future punishment, and to the Being and government of God. This, then, is certain: Because forever, when applied to some things, does not mean absolute eternity, it does not follow that it does not mean eternity when applied to future retribution. If it were so, we could not convey the idea of the eternity of God—for it could be said that forever is sometimes applied to a limited duration. This is true. Now, if this proves that future punishment is not forever, it must also prove that the Being of God is not forever. Two things are beyond dispute: First, Forever and everlasting are applied to future retributions. Second, These terms always mean the whole, as to duration, of that with which they stand connected. If applied to life, it is the whole of life; if to the existence of the world, it is the entire period of its existence; if to a covenant, the covenant is either without limit as to time, or it is the whole of the duration which the subject permits; and when applied to Jehovah, it refers to His whole eternity. What then does it mean when applied to future retribution; it always means the whole of something? Is it the whole of future existence? No one can base a denial of it on the ground that the word when applied to human life mean only a few years, or a limited duration when applied to the earth. For how is it when applied to God, and the happiness of heaven? It is certainly the place of any who deny endless retribution, to show that the words cannot mean the whole of future existence when applied by the use of the same Greek words in the same passages, to the happiness of the righteous. The objector must show that when applied to the future life they mean only a part, notwithstanding they always mean the whole of every thing else with which they stand connected."

And hence we find that those who deny that the words eternal and everlasting mean endless, when applied to the duration of the misery of the wicked beyond the grave to be consistent, maintain that the natural force of these words when applied to the duration of God's existence do not imply His endless existence.

So that in denying what God says concerning the endless misery of the wicked, they deny that what He says of the duration of His own existence proves that He will always exist. Alas, what infatuation, if not absolute Atheism, is here disclosed!

*10

Now, with these well established principles of interpreting the words eternal and forever as denoting the longest space of time possible in the nature of the case, let us adduce some Scriptural proof of the endless misery of all who die in their sins, impenitent and unbelieving. We learn in the Scriptures that " God spared not the angels that sinned, but cast them down to hell, and delivered them into chains of darkness, to be reserved unto judgment." And as "it is appointed unto men once to die, but after this the judgment," and " many of them that sleep in the dust of the earth shall awake, some to everlasting life and some to shame and everlasting contempt," "all that are in the graves shall hear His voice, and shall come forth; they that have done good, unto the resurrection of life; and they that have done evil, unto the resurrection of damnation."

So that it plainly appears that those who die without true repentance must come forth in the resurrection, and be condemned to punishment at the day of judgment. " Then shall our Lord say to those on His left hand, ' Depart from me, ye cursed, into everlasting fire, prepared for the devil and his angels.' And these shall go away into eternal punishment; but the righteous into life eternal." " He that believeth on the Son hath everlasting life; and he that believeth not the Son shall not see life, but the wrath of God abideth on him."

Now who can doubt that the Bible teaches the endless misery of the wicked after death, and that " they shall be tormented, day and night, forever and ever?"

# RETRIBUTION. 115

Rev. Albert Barnes thus shows the difficulty of being a Universalist and a Bible believer at the same time: "I could not embrace Universalism, with my views of the proper rules of interpreting language, without giving up the Bible altogether. The Bible does not teach the salvation of all men. It can never be made to teach that doctrine by a proper interpretation of language. If the Bible teaches anything clearly; if words have any meaning; if there are any proper rules of interpreting language, the Bible teaches the doctrine of the eternal punishment of the wicked, and it cannot be made to teach otherwise. I hold just what the mass of men have held; what ninety-nine men out of every hundred have held; what all men—Christians and infidels—except the small class who call themselves Universalists, have held, hat the Bible teaches that the wicked will be punished forever in the future world. If I were, therefore, to reject the doctrine of the future punishment of the wicked, I should not be a Universalist, trying to hold on to the Bible. I should become at once an honest infidel, and would reject the Bible altogether. The infidel is the only consistent man. I think in the view which I take of the fair interpretation of the Bible, that I see the reason why there are so few avowed Universalists, as compared with the actual number of infidels in our country, and why it is so difficult to keep up the system of Universalism as an organization. The number of persons in any community who can be made to believe that the Bible inculcates the doctrine of universal salvation must always be small; the number of those who, for various causes, reject it altogether, may be and probably will be much larger. Of the two I would be one of the latter, and so the mass of men do judge, and always will judge."

# CHAPTER XX.

## UNREASONABLENESS OF UNIVERSAL RESTORATION BY CHASTISEMENT AND DISCIPLINARY EDUCATION.

In the first place, I now propose to show that the proper administration of God's positive moral government over free moral agents, demands that eternal punishment should be the appropriate reward of a sinful life, in addition to the mere natural consequences of sin in the present world. I repeat the proposition, for its establishment seems to me adapted to refute the theory of mere natural consequences, the religion of Deism, and of two of the most popular heretical sects which have flourished especially in the vicinity of Boston, during the last half century. By natural consequences is meant, that when a man violates natural law, in thrusting his finger into a candle blaze, it burns, but ceases soon after it is withdrawn. And when a man violates God's moral law, he suffers the stings of conscience, which is all the punishment that the greatest sins deserve, or will receive. Our Creator has implanted within all the subjects of His moral government a moral constitution, by which we are made to discern the difference between right and wrong—by which we are made to recognize His moral law, and feel ourselves under the necessity of obeying or disobeying it.

And this conscience operating as God's vicegerent in the soul, in the performance of its disciplinary work, naturally imparts to us complacent satisfaction for well doing, and recriminates and censures us for violating what it dictates as right or as pleasing to God.

As the natural results of an honest and strenuous endeavor to glorify God, in obeying the moral law, in suppressing our unlawful propensities and selfish tendencies, we enjoy inward harmony and peace and are cheered by the consciousness of our heavenly Father's approval, while the natural results of wreckless disobedience to divine requirements, in yielding to the control of pernicious and debasing practices, are self-reproach and a consciousness of justly deserving the wrath of our offended Lord. But neither of these species of happiness or unhappiness, as the natural consequences of virtue and vice in the present life, I apprehend, can strictly be denominated rewards and penalties, for the chief reason for their employment seems to be the corrective guide or discipline of the individuals who experience them. Thus the natural effects of the approval and remonstrances of conscience, seem to be chiefly designed for personal guards against sin, and allurements to holiness.

The remonstrances of conscience are merely the

prickly thorns which project from the walls that are erected as hedges to guide the traveler in the way of duty—in the straight and narrow path toward heaven. These natural disciplinary chastisements are designed mainly to reclaim transgressors, while it is not the object of positive penal sanctions to secure reformation.

But as these incidental benefits of obedience, and evils of disobedience in this life, do not seem in the strictest sense to be of the nature of, rewards and penalties—not meeting our sense of the intrinsic demands of either retributive or public justice—we infer that they are wholly insufficient, and that God must exercise a positive moral government over free moral agents, which shall lead Him to award as a gift of His grace, eternal life to His friends, and inflict as just desert, eternal death upon His enemies. For no well regulated community feels satisfied that its most virtuous citizens are sufficiently rewarded for all their personal sacrifices in doing good, by merely an approving conscience, or that the most guilty are sufficiently punished by its reproaches. The community feel that the benefactors of the race, such as Washington and Lafayette, deserve from them some positive reward, and the scourges and criminals, such as Robespierre and Napoleon, deserve some positive punishment. The mass of men feel that devoted Christians must enjoy heaven hereafter, and the wicked must be consigned to hell.

But if we are satisfied that natural consequences are insufficient appendages to the moral law, and God must administer a positive moral government over men, let us inquire into its nature and sanctions.

God's positive moral government is the rightful authority, which He exercises over moral beings through the medium of His moral law. And this law must be the preceptive rule of action, for the guidance of moral agents, and it must have adequate sanctions to induce them to obey it. But it is not necessary to the perfection of moral government that it should actually secure unfaltering obedience. It is only necessary that it should have the most effective sanctions or motives, in the form of rewards and penalties for securing obedience, while men are left free and responsible in obeying or disobeying the law. But if this law were attended merely by natural consequences it would be self-executive, though God should cease to reign. If its violation incurs no positive governmental inflictions, it would degenerate into mere preceptive advice, and cease to be positive law. It would be a system of natural instead of revealed religion. But if every transgression and disobedience shall receive a just recompense of reward, the sanctions of the law must be executed by the Moral Governor himself.

Hence, the very idea of moral government implies that the law is not self-executive, without adequate penal sanctions, but in its very nature active and positive, demanding the constant enforcement of the authoritative Law-Giver. Therefore, if God does not administer a moral government, with adequate sanctions, He may have on the theory of natural consequences natural laws; but He can have no moral laws and no free moral agents under His direct control. And yet we know from the perfection of our

Creator's attributes, and from our own moral nature, that He is a perfect moral governor, with a perfect moral law, and with responsible subjects under His government whom He controls by appropriate sanctions. Now these adequate sanctions of His law are motives, rewards promised to obedience to its precepts, and penalties threatened against disobedience. And if God is a perfect moral governor, He must show by the extent and duration of these sanctions, that He regards obedience with supreme approval and disobedience with the greatest possible aversion.

But how can He manifest His supreme hatred to sin, as the worst thing in the universe, if He does not threaten the sinner with eternal punishment? If He does not inflict upon the transgressor eternal death as the appropriate penalty of a sinful life, He must weaken His authority and show that He regards the violation of His law as a less evil than the infliction of its penalty. In order to prevent to the utmost possible extent every transgression of His perfect law, the penalty must be as apalling as justice and the nature of the case will possibly admit, while it does not transcend in severity the intrinsic ill desert of each transgressor. In a perfect moral government distributive justice must be the standard by which the most terrific penalties of the law are awarded. The penalty upon each transgressor, being graduated by his intrinsic guilt, is as great as possible, and as the sinner is finite in his susceptibility of suffering, his punishment is as appalling as justice and the nature of the case will possibly admit, while it is finite in degree and endless in duration.

And while retributive justice both admits and demands this penalty, public justice—which is designed to secure the highest public good by securing the greatest amount and most perfect obedience to the divine law—insists that the soul that sinneth it shall die. And as every sin is against an infinite God, and a violation of a perfect law, it must involve infinite guilt in the sense of deserving eternal punishment.

# CHAPTER XXI.

## THE CONSISTENCY OF ETERNAL PUNISHMENT WITH GOD'S BENEVOLENCE AND GOODNESS.

(EXTRACT.)

All must admit that God manifests His love in creating men, and in giving them a perfectly good law which requires them to love Him with all their heart and one another as they love themselves. Is He not good, then, in offering the most glorious rewards to secure obedience, and in threatening transgressors with the most dreadful and deserved punishments? For certainly if He was good in making them rational and accountable creatures, and in giving them the best of laws, He must be equally good in maintaining obedience by the most effective motives. How long could His government stand, or His authority be received without them? Is not a human government just as benevolent and good in inflicting the death penalty upon the murderer as in rewarding her most faithful public servants with honor and emoluments of office? And, furthermore, does not God manifest His love in giving His only begotten Son, that whosoever believeth in Him should not perish but have everlasting life?

"No argument," says Dr. Hawes, "is more frequently urged by Universalists, or relied upon with greater confidence, than that derived from *the goodness of God*. They assert that the doctrine of future punishment is totally inconsistent with this attribute of the Deity. It is admitted on all hands that God is a being of infinite goodness. But what does this prove? That no evil natural or moral, can exist under the government of God; that all the subjects of His empire must be holy and happy? Look at facts. Has not sin existed on earth for six thousand years; and multiplied sorrow and pain and death to an almost inconceivable extent? Is all this consistent with the goodness of God? No Universalist, I suppose, will deny that it is. How then does he know that misery in the future world is not consistent with the same goodness? Guilty men, in the present life, often endure a great amount of suffering; why then may they not endure the same in the life to come? Is it said that temporal misery may be so overruled as to promote the *good* of God's creation on the whole? And why may not eternal misery? All that the goodness of God demands is, that he govern in such a manner as will secure the greatest amount of good in the universe. That great temporal sufferings are consistent with this, is proved by facts; and who but God is competent to decide that eternal sufferings are not?

Is it said that such sufferings inflicted as a punishment for sin are *unjust?* I ask again, who among the sons of men is qualified to decide this matter? Does any one know enough of God and His government to determine what laws He ought to enact, and what sanctions append to them? Can you see any injustice in God's leaving creatures who have voluntarily rebelled against Him, to continue in sin forever; and if they continue to sin forever, may not God justly punish them forever?

With a view to disprove the doctrine of future punishment, Universalists are very fond of *appealing to the sympathies of our nature, especially to parental feelings.* " What man," it is asked, " of common sensibility, could endure to see a fellow-man tormented in the fire or on the rack, for one year, or one month? What parent could take his own child and cast him into a glowing oven, or confine him in a gloomy dungeon for life? But has not God as much goodness as man; or as much kindness as an earthly parent? How then can it be supposed that he will cast any of His children into the lake of fire, and confine them there forever?" This is a very favorite argument with Universalists, and one which, with young and unthinking minds, they use with very great effect. But in reply, it may be asked; what parent would drown his children in the water, or consume them in the fire? What parent would break their bones, or mangle their flesh, or send upon them sickness and pain and death? And yet God, the great Parent of men, brings all these things upon them in the course of His providence. Has He then less kindness and love than earthly parents?

*11

# (4.) TRUE RELIGION.

## CHAPTER XXII.

### THE NATURE OF TRUE RELIGION BENEVOLENT, AND VOLUNTARY OBEDIENCE TO GOD NOT MERELY THE EXCITEMENT OF RIGHT FEELINGS.

The Bible teaches that true religion consists in genuine benevolence; in supreme love to God, and impartial love to men; in voluntary obedience to the Divne Law Giver, "for love is the fulfillment of the law;" "In such genuine repentance toward God, and faith toward our Lord Jesus Christ, as purifies the heart and overcomes the temptations of the world, the flesh, and the devil." For Jesus, the Divine founder of the Christian religion, said: "Thou shalt love the Lord thy God with all thy heart, and with all thy soul, and with all thy mind." This is the first and great commandment, and the second is like unto it—" Thou shalt love thy neighbor as thyself." On these two commandments hang all the law and the prophets. "Fear God and keep His commandments, for this is the whole duty of man." "Repent ye, and believe the gospel." "Believe on the Lord Jesus Christ, and thou shalt be saved." "For with the heart man believeth unto righteousness."

But with these divine commands and instructions, showing that love—including voluntary obedience to God's requirements—constitute the nature of the Christian religion, a very common and dangerous error seems to prevail in reference to this fundamental truth. Very many persons, if we understand them correctly, believe and maintain that true religion consists in the excitement of the sensibilities, feelings, emotions, and desires, in connection with the worship of God. They seem to believe and teach that happy frames of mind, with right feelings, constitute the nature of the religion of Christ. Therefore, when their feelings become pleasantly excited, in connection with sympathetic and social religious worship, they consider themselves very religious, and that they really enjoy what they regard true religion. But when engaged in the wearisome, and often vexatious, employments of daily life, and the natural reaction follows from the previous excitement of their feelings—so that natural mental depression and sluggishness are experienced—they regard themselves in a back-slidden state, suffering the frowns of their Heavenly Father.

This mistake in believing that the excitement of what they consider to be right feelings, is religion, is the cause of the frequent gloom and despondency of conscientious persons.

"By false views concerning the nature of true religion," as a writer has observed, "many real Christians have been stumbled and kept in bondage, and their comfort and usefulness much abridged by finding themselves from time to time very languid and unfeeling. Supposing religion to consist in right and exciting feelings, if at any time the excitability of the sensibility becomes exhausted and their feelings subside, they are immediately thrown into unbelief and bondage. Satan reproaches them for the want of feeling, and they have nothing to say only to admit the truth of his accusations. Having a false philosophy of religion, they judge of the state of their hearts by the state of their feelings. They confound their hearts with their feelings, and are in almost constant perplexity to keep their hearts right, by which they mean their feelings in a state of excitement."

Persons with such desponding and gloomy experiences, as Dr. Payson and David Brainard, suffer greatly from their erroneous belief on this point. Sometimes they feel languid and are conscious of classes of emotions which they falsely call sins. These they earnestly resist, and still blame themselves for having them in their hearts, as they say. Thus they are brought again into bondage, although they are certain that these feelings are hated, and not at all indulged by them.

Another injurious result of mistaking mere feelings for true religion, is found in the fact that persons anxiously inquiring the way of salvation know not how to excite their feelings so as to become

Christians. Finding that their feelings are but very slightly if at all under the control of the voluntary powers, they soon become discouraged in seeking to become religious, and abandon all efforts to become Christians. As the result, the Holy Spirit is grieved away, and they return to carelessness on the subject of religion.

Now the injurious error of Christians suffering with gloomy and morbid experiences, as well as the error of anxious inquirers for the way of salvation under the special strivings of the Holy Spirit, may be in a great measure corrected by considering that the divine law does not so much demand right feeling, as right, willing, voluntary love and obedience to God. The Bible appeals directly and repeatedly to the voluntary powers, but very indirectly, if at all, to our mere feelings. And sound intellectual and moral philosophy supports the reasonableness of such appeals and claims of the Bible.

Although the human mind is essentially one in its essence and being, yet it exists in three diverse compartments: Intellect, Sensibility, or Feeling, and the Will. The intellect perceives, but the will is only the main subject of moral law, and is supreme in its indirect control of all the other powers of the mind. The feelings, in themselves, seem to have little or no moral character, while the will regulates all our voluntary actions whether right or wrong.

Hence the divine appeal to the will, "Choose this day whom ye will serve," while there is no command "excite your feelings."

According to the Scriptures all mankind are by nature children of wrath, dead in trespasses and sin. All their sin consists in sinning. They strive voluntarily to gratify their natural propensities in preference to pleasing God. Therefore their sin consists in their voluntary neglect of obedience to the divine commands, or in voluntary disobedience to the divine laws. Hence their sin cannot consist in mere feeling, but in wrong voluntary omission of the divine requirements, or in positive voluntary transgression of God's holy law. And as all men by nature are prone to indulge themselves in absolute and habitual transgression, none can be saved by their own personal righteousness, but by the mercy of God, by the washing of regeneration, and renewing of the Holy Ghost. But in this radical change, from seeking to please themselves supremely, to voluntarily pleasing God, they are free and responsible, while God makes them willing in the day of His power. He commands sinners to do their duty in reference to this great change, and declares that He is ever ready to save them by His grace. The Lord is not willing that any should perish, but that all should come to repentance.

Religious experience, in the sinner's change from serving the world to the service of God, consists of two parts—the duty part, that which the sinner must render, which of course is a right state of the will towards God, and the experience part, which includes the emotional exercises, naturally attending and flowing from this state of the will—and also any movement of thought or feeling, which comes from God's response to the voluntary surrender of the soul to Him. These statements seem to be taught in the

Bible. There God says: "Behold, I stand at the door, and knock. If any man hear my voice, and open the door, I will come into him, and will sup with him and he with Me."

Thus we perceive that religious experience involves the whole heart; our duty, the requirements of religion, is to hear his voice and open the door. All the rest God takes care of, in renewing and sanctifying, and saving the sinner.

God says to all sinners, "Repent, and turn yourselves from all your transgressions, so iniquity shall not be your ruin, and make you a new heart and a new spirit, for why will ye die?" And this seems to mean, make a radical voluntary change in the moral affections and ruling intentions of the mind from sinful gratification to holy obedience to God. The guilt of all impenitent sinners, is in their unwillingness to love and serve God. Jesus says "Ye will not come to me that ye might have life." Unwillingness is the single reason why all unregenerate sinners are not Christians. God says, "Believe on the Lord Jesus Christ, and thou shalt be saved." Jesus says, "Come unto me and I will give you rest. Learn of me, for I am meek and lowly in heart. I will put a new song in thy mouth, even praise unto our God. A new heart also will I give you, and a new spirit will I put within you, and cause you to walk in my statutes." And from such divine teachings as these it seems to me very plain that the nature of true religion consists in benevolent and voluntary obedience to God, and not merely in the excitement of right feeling toward Him and our fellow-men.

# CHAPTER XXIII.

## THE SERVICE OF THE LORD IN SECULAR DUTIES.

It is common, even among professing Christians, to dissociate in their minds, too widely the worship of God, and strictly religious services, from the practical and ordinary secular duties of life. Hence they frequently perform their secular duties without regulating them by a religious spirit, in obedience to the divine commands.

They think of preaching, prayer, praise and exhortation, as specially religious and pleasing to God; forgetting that the benevolent and honest performance of all their secular duties, at appropriate times and places, are also, if not equally essential, as fundamental indications of true and accepted piety toward God. For He has said, "Whether, therefore, ye eat or drink, or whatsoever ye do, do all to the glory of God." Let it be your ruling motive in all your plans and actions, to seek supremely the honor of your heavenly Father, as your Creator, Law-giver, Redeemer and Judge.

Let your example and precept be such as to honor God, and influence others to embrace and practice the principles of the gospel of Christ. The true Christian must aim to glorify God in all his ordinary business affairs.

He is bound to make it manifest to all observers, that his secular business is designed and adapted, not merely to benefit himself, but with a benevolent spirit and strict honesty, to promote the welfare of his fellow-men. He is not at liberty to pursue any vocation which is naturally detrimental to society, lest he misrepresent and dishonor religion Therefore it becomes all Christians to so arrange their domestic affairs, their houses, their furniture and equipage as to glorify God.

They are to "use this world as not abusing it," in all their relations to it. They are to furnish their tables with such agreeable and healthful food and drink, and partake of them in such a temperate manner, as shall subserve their efficiency and usefulness, not only in their more strictly religious duties, as commonly understood, but also in the common secular affairs of life. As a writer has observed; "It is generally conceded that the work of forming character, of directing the plastic minds of children is of the utmost importance.

If it were better understood and conscientiously performed, adult life would not so often be a long and agonizing struggle between conscience and evil desires, and evil would be found hateful and not in accordance with habit.

As the character therefore acquired in this life must

materially affect our condition in the life beyond this one, it would seem that mothers and teachers have especially committed to them the work of the Lord." As without the earnings of husbands and fathers, women would have to be bread-providers when helpless little ones make exhausting demands upon their souls and bodies, thus of necessity discharging imperfectly two separate and conflicting lines of duty. The work of men in business is also seen to be a part of the Lord's work.

Inasmuch as patriotism has in all ages been considered one of the most exalted duties of man, and no land can long be, even in a low degree, prosperous, whose laws are not based on justice—the exercise of political duties must also be a part of the work of the Lord. Well would it be for our country if all professing Christians, as well as educated men, more generally recognized and acted upon this truth.

Reforms have a vital connection with the moral and spiritual development of nations, and must therefore be an important part of the work of the Lord. The habit of thinking of religious duty as though it did not embrace, and had no necessary connection with the secular affairs of life, but might be all performed at particular places and seasons; that nothing but the promulgation or acceptance of doctrinal truth, and the public or private exercises of worship can be properly called the work of the Lord, is most pernicious.

Its tendency is to make Christians feel that the domestic, educational and business duties of life, when performed even with an eye single to the glory of God, are so secular and worldly that they cannot be religiously regulated, so as to ensure the divine commendation: " Well done, good and faithful servant, enter thou into the joy of thy Lord."

# CHAPTER XXIV.

## WHO ARE THE RIGHTEOUS?

There is a distinction between saints and sinners, but it is very common for men to estimate themselves and their associates in proportion to their external morality, or the apparent strictness of their religious and ceremonial observances, so as to think that their infinitesimal differences can form no clear line of distinction between living Christians and the very best of mere moralists. But " the Lord (who) searcheth all hearts, and understandeth all the imaginations of the thoughts," clearly discerns a very wide and radical distinction between the habitual and ruling intentions of the most inconsistent of the real imitators of their Divine Master, and the most upright of mere worldlings, who follow their natural desires, in pleasing themselves rather than making it their supreme and all controlling purpose to please their Heavenly Father in all things. Hence it becomes us to study the Scriptures carefully, that we may understand the fundamental difference between those whom God denominates "the righteous and the wicked, and those who serve God and those who serve Him not."

Who then are the righteous? In the Bible we learn that the righteous are not those who with the boastful spirit of the Pharisees, " trust in themselves that they are righteous, and despise others." " For every one that exalteth himself shall be abased." They do not trust in their good works, " knowing that a man is not justified by the works of the law, but by the faith of Jesus Christ." And they have no confidence in the saving efficacy of the mere heartless forms and ceremonials of religion. For God says to all such devotees at His altars, " Bring no more oblation; incense is an abomination unto me. The new moons and Sabbaths, and the calling of assemblies, I cannot away with; it is iniquity, even the solemn meeting. Behold, to obey is better than sacrifice." Neither do the truly righteous trust to their excited feelings and emotional exercises as proof in itself of their Christian character. If any, at the time of their hopeful conversion are mistaken, so as to consider mere animal excitement religion, they will soon discover when it subsides that " they have no root in themselves, and so endure but for a time; afterward, when affliction or persecution ariseth, for the world's sake immediately they are offended, and abandon their spurious hopes of heaven."

But I now maintain affirmatively that the righteous are those who have renounced mere self-gratification as their uniform law, and have given themselves up devotedly to obey the divine law, as revealed in the conscience enlightened by the illumination of God's Holy word.

They abandon their native selfishness, and under the operations of the Holy Spirit they honestly and perseveringly endeavor to live a life of supreme and benevolent love to God and impartial love to men, so that like Jesus, their Almighty Saviour and guide, they may go about doing good to friends and foes.

#### EXTRACTS.

(1) Now do any think that such a benevolent state of mind as this would require us to treat all other interests of equal value with our own? No 'man does or can act upon such a principle, which would lead to the neglect of the things especially committed to our care. God has never acted upon such a principle. He has always acted upon the principle of accomplishing the greatest practicable good. He esteems the good of all and of each of His creatures, according to their intrinsic and relative value, but exercises His own discretion in His efforts to accomplish the greatest amount of good. And such must be the course of all truly benevolent Christians. For "if any provide not for his own, and especially for those of his own house, he hath denied the faith and is worse than an infidel." "Let us not be weary in well doing; for in due season we shall reap if we faint not." "As we have therefore opportunity, let us do good unto all men, especially unto them who are of the household of faith." The greatest practical good must be the aim of the true Christian. He

must bestow his particular efforts, influence, and possession, upon those particular interests and persons, where on the whole he thinks it will do the greatest amount of good.

(2) The true saint is justified by faith in Christ, and has the evidence of it in the peace of his own mind. He is conscious of obeying the law of reason and of love. He has also within him the Spirit of God, witnessing with his spirit that he is a child of God, forgiven, accepted, and adopted. He is conscious that he pleases God and has His approbation.

(3) But further, the true Christian overcomes the temptations of the world. "For whatsoever is born of God, overcometh the world; and this is the victory that overcometh the world, even our faith." And hereby we know Him, if "we keep His commandments, and His commandments are not grevious."

(4) And overcoming the world implies overcoming as far as practicable, in our feeble condition, all needless anxiety concerning our worldly affairs. It is perfectly natural for worldly-minded and selfish men to set their affections on attaining a great amount of worldly property, and they have not learned that while prudent and industrious they should trust God to give or withhold, according to His unerring wisdom. Hence their bosoms are like the "troubled sea, that cannot rest." But the faithful and devoted Christian, who sets his "affections on things above, and not supremely on the fading things of earth," gets above the world, to a great extent, and is freed from ceaseless and corroding anxiety. "For God doeth all things well."

(5) The true saint is, also, a reformer from principle. He is distinguished by his firm adherence to all the principles and rules of the divine government. He needs not the gale of popular excitement or of popular applause to put and keep him in motion. His intellect and conscience have taken the control of his will, so that he seeks divine grace not only to reform himself, but strives to reform as he has opportunity all the existing evils of society. He sympathizes with every effort to reform mankind and promote the interests of truth and righteousness in the earth.

(6) Christians have the spirit of Christ. "What, know ye not that your body is the temple of the Holy Ghost which is in you, which ye have of God, and ye are not your own? But ye are not in the flesh, but in the spirit, if so be that the Spirit of God dwell in you. Now, if any man have not the Spirit of Christ, he is none of His. And if Christ be in you the body is dead because of sin; but the Spirit is life, because of righteousness. The fruit of the Spirit is love, joy, peace, long suffering, gentleness, goodness, faith, meekness, temperance." They that are Christ's, have crucified the flesh with the affections and lusts.

(7) Christians, or truly regenerate souls, experience great and present blessedness in religion. They do not seek their own happiness as their supreme good, but find it in their disinterested efforts to promote the well being of others. Their state of mind is itself the harmony of the soul. Happiness is both a natural result of virtue and also its governmental reward. Christians enjoy religion just for the reason

that they are disinterested in it; that is, precisely for the reason that their own enjoyment is not the end which they seek. And selfish professors do not enjoy their religion, just for the reason that their own enjoyment is the end at which they aim. But if I seek the good of others, I have the approbation of conscience, and conscious communion and fellowship with God.

Finally, I observe our natural birth, with its attendant laws of physical and mental development, becomes the occasion of our bondage to sin and suffering in this world. Right over against this lies the birth into the kingdom of God, by the spirit. By this the soul is brought into new relations, into intimate contact, with spiritual things. The Spirit of God seems to usher the soul into the spiritual world, in a manner strictly analogous to the results of the natural birth upon our physical being. The great truths of the spiritual world are opened to our view through the illumination of the Spirit of God; we seem to see with new eyes, and to have a new world of spiritual objects around us.

# CHAPTER XXV.

## DIFFERENCE BETWEEN MORALITY AND RELIGION.

Morality in the common acceptation of the term, denotes that system of moral duties which men owe to each other in their natural and social relations. It refers to their external actions as they bear upon the relative rights and welfare of each other, and thus it determines their conduct to be right in their treatment and intercourse with each other.

In this common use of the term, it applies to actions which merely accord with justice and human laws, without reference to the motives from which they proceed. But the term religion, from the Latin, to reconsider, to bind anew, to fasten, consists in rebinding a sinner to God, who has been separated from Him.

Hence religion not only ensures the practice of the moral virtues towards men, but demands a much higher and stricter type of morality, which is regulated by supreme love to God and an internal design to obey all His holy requirements, in worshiping Him and doing good to all classes of the human family.

Hence religion is distinct from mere morality as the latter word is commonly employed, and consists in the performance of the duties we owe directly to God, from a principle of obedience to His holy law.

Says Rev. Joseph Cook, " That the ancients understood the difference between morality and religion is evident from the statement that Ulysses passing the enchanted island, filled the ears of his crew with wax and tying himself with knotted cords to the mast, that the voice of the Sirens might not attract them to the shore. Orpheus who followed, furnished better music than the Sirens, and the temptation was removed."

"Morality," says Mr. Cook, " is a selfish bond of knotted cords, a selfish slavishness, where a person wishes to sin and dares not. Religion is the obedience of affectionate gladness. The Christian is a man who changes eyes with God. He regards sin in all its forms as God does. When a man has acquired good and can practice it, and practice it as the pleasing and controlling purpose of his life, it is good proof that it is genuine. If when face to face with temptation we can do this, it is good evidence. Religion, therefore, and not mere morality is necessary to the soul's peace. The moral man knows that if he puts his hand in the fire he will burn it. ' The fear of the Lord is the beginning of wisdom.' The love of the Lord is of little value, and cannot be genuine if there is no fear in the heart. We must delight in all the attributes of God, His justice, as well as His mercy, or we cannot be genuine Christians. He who in sailing past the island of temptation, has enlightened selfishness enough not to land, although he rather wants to,—he who therefore binds himself to the mast with knotted thongs, and fills the ears of his crew with wax ; he who does this, without hearing a better music is the man of mere morality. In facing sirens, thongs are good but songs are better. When a man of tempestuous, unrestrained spirit must sail over amber and azure and purple seas, past the island of the Sirens, and knots himself to the mast of mere outwardly right conduct, by the thongs of safe resolutions, although as yet duty is not his delight, he is near to virtue. He who spake as never mortal man spoke, saw such a young man once, and looking on him, loved him, and yet said, as the nature of things says also, 'one thing thou lackest' Evidently he to whom duty is not a delight, does not possess the supreme pre-requisite to peace and Christian acceptance and fellowship with his Master. Morality is Ulysses bound to the mast. Religion is Orpheus listening to a better melody, and passing with disdain the sorceress' shore."

# CHAPTER XXVI.

## THE MERE MORALIST GUILTY AND CONDEMNED.

It is common for men to estimate their innocence and guilt by the strictness or defects of their external morality. Hence they do not readily perceive the radical and wide difference "between the righteous and the wicked; between him that serveth God and him that serveth Him not." Judging according to outward appearances merely, it seems to them that there can be no such essential and wide difference between the best of moralists and the most defective of genuine Christians, as shall not only separate them widely here, in the estimation of the searcher of hearts, but also separate them forever, by a bridgeless gulf in the future world. But they should remember that "the Lord seeth not as man seeth; for man looketh on the outward appearance, but the Lord looketh on the heart."

The Lord sees that the strictest of mere moralists, in all his natural amiability and correctness of deportment, seeks uniformly to follow the natural inclinations of his unrenewed heart, in doing that which is pleasing to himself, without supreme regard to the commands and pleasure of his Creator, who not only forbids all evil, in thought, word and deed, but goes further and demands positive obedience and intentional service. " Whether therefore ye eat or drink, or whatsoever ye do, do all to the glory of God." With supreme love to God in the heart, there must be an habitual purpose to please Him in all the ordinary pursuits of life. But the strictest of unregenerate moralists, are conscious that they are not governed uniformly by such a controlling motive.

And our Lord when on earth said of this class of mere moralists, " I know you, that you have not the love of God in you." Hence they are guilty and condemned for the want of love to God, for the neglect of duty, and for sins of omission. The sin of the mere moralist results mainly from his defective intention. " For all have sinned and come short of the glory of God." "He that is not with me (says our Lord) is against me." But the Christian is penitent for the sin of omission, while the mere moralist is impenitent. The moralist is not changed and renewed in the ruling purposes of his heart. Even though his outward life be free from reproach, his controlling intention is not the divine glory. While not loving God supremely, and manifesting His love by designing to please Him in all things, his outward conduct, however commendable abstractly, does not meet the claims of the moral law. For " love is the fulfilling of the law." While with the true Christian, he may favor by his presence and support public worship, he is not a spiritual worshiper from the heart. He does not meet the claims of the divine command. For God has said, " they that worship Him must worship Him in spirit and in truth," and " Him only shalt thou serve." " For they that are after the flesh do mind the things of the flesh ; but they that are after the spirit, the things of the spirit. So then they that are in the flesh cannot please God. Thou art weighed in the balance and found wanting."

# CHAPTER XXVII.

## HUMILITY AND SELF ESTIMATION.

True humility consists in a modest and correct estimate of our individual worth in comparison with others. It does not require us to entertain a lower opinion of ourselves than we really deserve. If with good reasons we know ourselves to be possessed of a good measure of talent, intelligence and virtue, we have no right to consider ourselves inferior to those who possess in reality less of these qualities.

But genuine humility does not consist in a low opinion of ourselves in comparison with God, and in not attributing to ourselves any excellence or attainments which we do not possess. Hence the divine requirement, " Be clothed with humility, for God resisteth the proud and giveth grace to the humble." Let not a man " think of himself more highly than he ought to think," but let him think soberly, reasonably, in conformity with facts and things, as they really exist. It cannot be wrong for a man to esteem himself more skillful in his profession or trade, than some of his brethren if he really is so. Such an estimate is not incompatible with true humility. If a man finds that on the whole, his mind is more active, and his opportunities for information have been greater than the mass of men, he is justifiable in believing the facts in the case. If a man is conscious of clearness and logical accuracy in reasoning, and fluency of speech, humility cannot require him to disbelieve the facts, lest he be considered "self-conceited, in thinking of himself more highly than he ought to think." But it is in religious matters, in the relation of men to God, that they are in special danger of entertaining radically dangerous and false opinions of their own goodness and the excellency of their conduct. These erroneous, as well as correct opinions, are forcibly illustrated by the prayers of the Pharisee and Publican, in our Lord's parable. "He spake this parable to certain ones who trusted in themselves that they were righteous." The Pharisee with a self-righteous spirit, thanked God that he was "not as other men are." He professed to abstain from wrong doing to others, and maintained that he strictly observed all religious ceremonies. He relied upon this kind of righteousness, and therefore he made public and ostentatious professions of his own goodness. Such a standard of estimate was "abominable in the sight of God, who looks into the heart, and who sees wickedness there, when the external actions may be blameless." But the Publican had a more correct estimate of himself. He was conscious of his guilt and ill-desert. He was grieved in view of his sins, and was ready to humbly confess them to God. Hence his penitential prayer, " God be merciful to me a sinner." I tell you this man went down to his house justified, rather than the other. " For every one that exalteth himself shall be abased, and he that humbleth himself shall be exalted."

Says D. L. Moody, the wonderful revival preacher, " Now the difference between the Pharisee and Publican was, that one prayed in his own self-righteousness, and went away empty; the other did not bring his righteousness and good deeds, but brought his sins. The Pharisee came full of pride; he wanted religion and God to bless him. God had a blessing in heaven for him, but He could not give it to him because he had no room to receive it, he was so full of conceit, full of self-righteousness of himself. In his mistaken self exaltation he was like the professing Christian in Revelation, who said, 'I am rich, and increased with goods, and have need of nothing.' Now self-righteous moralists, who in their secret thoughts, if not in their boasting professions, hope to be saved by their good works, may see their true character reflected in this divine looking-glass, and learn the folly and wickedness of their proud hearts. They cannot see the vileness of their own self righteousness. For 'we are all as an unclean thing, and all our righteousnesses are as filthy rags.' If we are really convicted, and see our sins as God does, we shall be truly penitent, and offer the prayer of the broken hearted Publican, ' God be merciful to me a sinner.' If with penitence we confess and forsake our sins, trusting in Christ who died for our sins, we shall have mercy. For such a correct and humble estimate of ourselves as ruined sinners, will lead us to offer unto God acceptable prayer, that we may be 'justified in His sight.' ' Verily I say unto you, except ye be converted and become as little children, ye shall not enter the kingdom of heaven.' ' For I say through the grace given unto me, to every man that is among you, not to think of himself more highly than he ought to think.' In lowliness of mind, let each esteem others better than themselves. Let this mind be in you, which was also in Christ Jesus."

# CHAPTER XXVIII.

### FULL ASSURANCE AND WITNESS OF THE SPIRIT.

" Faith is the milk," says Spurgeon, " and assurance is the cream that rises on it. If you have genuine milk you are pretty certain to have cream."

" There are two kinds or shades of assurance," says Dr. Cuyler, "one of faith, and one which the apostle calls the ' full assurance of hope.' Faith is the soul trusting itself to Jesus Christ. Assurance is the full confidence of a believer in his own safety— that being united to Christ, he is delivered from the law of sin and death."

" The spirit itself beareth witness with our spirit, that we are the children of God." Now in order to obtain this witness of the spirit, we must examine ourselves and see if the fruits of the spirit manifest themselves in our own experience. " The fruit of the spirit is love, joy, peace, long-suffering, gentleness, goodness, faith, meekness, temperance ; " against such there is no law. "They that are Christ's have crucified the flesh with the affections and lusts." The Christian who enjoys these fruits of the spirit has the inward witness of the spirit, and has a right to the full assurance of faith, of hope, and of understanding.

# CHAPTER XXIX.

## THE WAY OF EMINENT HOLINESS.

All true Christians are in some measure holy, and they desire an increase of holiness. And in proportion to their belief that entire holiness, either as an act or a state, is attainable in this life, they desire not only to be perfectly holy, but permanently so, that they may be completely fitted for the perfect society of the "spirits of just men, made perfect in heaven." Such holiness in men consists in entire conformity to the perfect moral character of God, and an earnest intention to do continually all his requirements, as well as to submit readily and unconditionally to all his dispensations, according to the ability and grace given unto us. How then shall we attain to this highest degree of holiness possible to men? Jesus saith, "I am the way, the truth, and the life." We must therefore not only consecrate ourselves entirely to His service, but we must abandon all trust in our own unaided strength to overcome temptation to sin, and trust entirely in the Lord Jesus Christ for victory. His name is called "Jesus, for He shall save His people from their sins." Says the apostle, "I can do all things through Christ which strengtheneth me." "This is the victory that overcometh the world, even our faith." Our Saviour has said to those who earnestly and persistently resist temptation, trusting to His assisting grace for purity of heart and victory over temptation, "Sin shall not have dominion over you, for ye are not under law but under grace." "He will not suffer you to be tempted above that ye are able, but with the temptation will make a way of escape that ye may be able to bear it." So that we may reckon ourselves "to be dead indeed unto sin, but alive unto God through Jesus Christ our Lord."

Then, in the words of an ancient saint hungering and thirsting after righteousness, we may say to Him in prayer, "Lord, thou hast declared that sin shall not have dominion over those that trust in Thee, for overcoming power and grace. I believe this word of Thine cannot be broken, and therefore, helpless in myself, I rely upon thy faithfulness to save me from the dominion of sins which now tempt me. Put forth thy power, O Lord Jesus Christ, and get Thyself great glory in subduing my flesh, with its affections and lusts." Then we must believe that our prayer will be answered, and we must leave ourselves in His care. "The blood of Jesus Christ cleanseth us from all sin," past and present, while the Holy Ghost, who is distinctively the sanctifier, applies the truth of Jesus in giving victory over temptation to sin. "Sanctify them through Thy truth." But the Comforter, which is the Holy Ghost, whom "the Father will send in my name, He shall teach you all things and bring all things to your remembrance, whatsoever I have said unto you."

If we trust Christ, moment by moment, for the fulfillment of His precious promises, the Holy Spirit will bring such weighty motives to our minds in favor of obedience to the divine law, that we shall experience their power to save. Then we shall be able to say:

> " 'Tis done!
> Thou dost this moment save,
> With full salvation bless,
> Redemption through the blood I have
> And spotless love and peace."

It will then be our habitual purpose to imitate the example of Christ in all our ways. It will be our strong desire that His spirit shall continually reign in our hearts, and control all our intentions as well as actions, and that we may have the same temper and disposition which actuated Him, and that we may have constantly in view the same great end which influenced our blessed Redeemer in His holy life.

## CHAPTER XXX.

### THE HIGHEST PRACTICAL PIETY.

(1.) SANCTIFICATION IMPORTANT.

In the early part of the present century, that eminent statesman and Christian philanthropist, William Wilberforce, of Great Britain, published a treatise of great religious value, on Practical Piety, which was widely circulated in Europe and America, and did more in elevating the standard of practical godliness throughout christendom than almost any other religious publication of that period. But during the more than half a century since that precious volume wrought its great religious reformation among the professed children of God, the facilities for propagating the Christian religion and enlightened civilization throughout the world, have increased more rapidly than at any previous period since its first promulgation. And as progress in science and the mechanic arts, and facilities for travel and intellectual intercommunication, with advantages for thorough general education, have increased in a more rapid ratio than in any previous period of our world's history, he who shall publish the most scriptural and acceptable explanation and method of attaining the highest state of practical piety, possible in the present life, on the part of Christians, may justly be considered not only a Christian, but a public benefactor. For the stirring aspect of the times, and the increased activities of the Christian life, imperatively demand the humblest as well as the most reflective and devout practical piety. But in presenting a theory for Christian living, for the children of God, it is obvious that it should be neither higher nor lower than the Bible imperatively requires, nor than is attainable as a matter of fact, in the Christian experience of every regenerated soul, who honestly and earnestly desires such an inestimable blessing, by the proffered aids of divine grace, however feeble may be his natural capacities, and however depraved may have been his natural propensities, and however formidable may be his struggles with outward temptation.

In view of the very low and superficial type of piety, which so commonly prevails among too many professing Chistians in our times, it is important that they realize not only their imperative duty and exalted privilege to attain the higher Christian life, but really to make the very highest practical attainments in scriptural holiness; that they should diligently aim at an endeavor to attain, and as their rule of life live, in a state of entire sanctification. Therefore, they should strive to the utmost practical extent by faith in Jesus Christ, to imitate "His example, who did no sin," and thus resist and overcome habitually the temptations to sin, from "the world, the flesh, and the devil." For in our Saviour's memorable intercessory prayer for all Christians, as He was about to terminate this mortal life, he said: "They are not of the world, even as I am not of the world. I pray not that Thou shouldst take them out of the world, but that Thou shouldst keep them from the evil. Sanctify them through Thy truth." Meaning that God should keep them from yielding to the temptations of the evil one, that is, the devil, from backsliding in heart, and from the slightest apostacy from a life of perfect purity and holiness, and that he would keep them cleansed from all sin.

(2) A REFORMATION GREATLY NEEDED.

But as this vital doctrine concerning the eminent personal holiness of the children of God, which occupied so prominent a place in the thoughts and desires of the blessed Master in His closing prayer on earth, has fallen into comparative obscurity in the prayers and exhortations of the mass of professing Christians, and is now almost as much neglected (if not absolutely discredited as impracticable,) as a matter of absolute Christian experience by many in the Protestant Christian Church, as the doctrine of justification by faith alone is, in the Papal Church; and, as we had a general reformation on the doctrine of justification by faith, about three and a half centuries ago, we as much need a more extensive one now, in the Protestant Church, on the doctrine of sanctification by faith in Jesus Christ. And as our Lord has said much more in the Scriptures in favor of entire sanctification in this life, than of justification, it is reasonable that His ministers should follow His example.

It is therefore for the want of this general reformation in the Church at large, in her teachings and efforts in promoting the highest form of practical holiness, that young converts enter the Church expecting to fall from their first love—or merely keep up a sufficient form of Godliness to retain their hope of salvation—instead of "growing in grace, and in the knowledge of our Lord and Saviour Jesus Christ."

And the low and worldly type of piety, prevailing as a natural consequence among many of our church-members, proves a formidable hindrance to success in preaching and other efforts for the conversion of sinners. The inconsistencies of such merely justified Christians, in the legal aspect of justification, so misrepresent the religion of Christ, to the impenitent, that they think a conversion to such a type of piety can hardly ensure their salvation; and their want of active co-operation in the service of God, and faithful co-operation with the ministry, too frequently paralyzes the effect of the most eloquent preaching.

Under such circumstances, it seems expedient in this connection, in a comprehensive manner, to define and vindicate this much neglected and vital Scripture truth, as taught by Christ and His apostles. It is certainly desirable that all Christians, and religious teachers especially, should entertain clear and consistent, as well as settled views, of this great cardinal and fundamental doctrine.

For our Saviour esteemed it so very important that He made the sanctification of His people the burden of His prayer under the most solemn circumstances. "That they all may be one, as thou, Father, art in me, and I in thee, that they may be one in us, that the world may believe that thou has sent me. I in them and thou in me, that they may be made perfect in one, and that the world may know that thou hast sent me." And from this we learn that all Christians should be perfectly united with Christ and each other in their plans, counsels and holy purposes in life, so as to reflect as in a mirror the very image of their Lord. For He hath said, "let your light shine before men, that they may see your good works, and Glorify your Father which is in Heaven."

Having considered in these prefatory statements, the importance of the Highest Practical Piety, and that a reformation is needed, to save misapprehension on the part of such persons, as may not have thoroughly and candidly studied the doctrine of practical holiness, it is of vital consequence that the following explanations should be clearly understood before the proof of its actual attainability can be fairly appreciated.

(3) DEFINITION.

"Sanctification is commonly defined to be that glorious work of God's free grace in the soul, by which a sinner after he has been justified, is renewed after the image of God and enabled to die unto sin and live unto righteousness."

Entire sanctification in this life, consists in entire

*14

conformity in heart and life to all the known will of God, in doing as well as a person can, or knows how to live. And this is all God requires. Entire consecration is essential to the commencement of the Christian life, "for whosoever he be of you," says the Master, "that forsaketh not all that he hath, he cannot be my disciple." He must "believe with the heart unto righteousness," in order to justification by faith in Christ. And being thus entirely consecrated, so far as this single act is concerned, he is entirely sanctified for the time being, for "the blood of Jesus Christ cleanseth us from all sin."

But in order that he may attain a state of entire sanctification, he must uniformly and continuously cherish entire purity of intention, dedicating his whole life to the love and service of God, by faith not only in the justifying but sanctifying grace of Jesus Christ. And such a life is lived in a state of entire and continuous sanctification. The prayer of faith, under the direction of the Holy Ghost, "the very God of peace sanctify you wholly, and preserve you blameless," is an aspiration for the most complete type of Christian character attainable in this life.

But the realization of such blameless piety in the eyes of the searcher of hearts, cannot reasonably be expected to render the Christian either omniscient or infallible, so as to exempt him from mistakes or even positive faults in the "judgment of men, who look upon the outward appearance, while the Lord looketh upon the heart," and judges by its purity of intention. For in fulfilling the apostle Paul's inspired prayer, "sanctify you wholly, and preserve you blameless,"

God can only sanctify the Christian and perpetuate his singleness of purpose, in resisting all temptation, and his fixed purpose to obey from the heart all the divine commandments.

The Christian therefore may be entirely sanctified in this life and be preserved blameless, even while he is not perfectly faultless in all his external conduct.

But does any one ask how this statement and distinction may appear consistent? Suffer me to borrow an illustration. "We may take a little child (says Miss Smiley) whose loving heart is bent on pleasing her mother. Her first little task of needle work is put into her hands, but the little fingers are all unskilled, nor has she any thought of the nicety required; and the mother, in taking it, sees two things; one is a work (really faulty) with the stitches long and crooked; and the other is that smiling, upturned face, with its sweetness of conscious love. The child is blameless, but her work not faultless. It will be nearer and nearer faultless as day after day she gathers skill, and ever new ideas of care and faithfulness in her tasks; but still in her mother's eyes she is, first as well as last, her blameless child, for she appreciates the earnestness and singleness of the intention in doing the work as well as it is possible with her feeble capacities. And surely every believing loving child of God may regard this blessing of blamelessness not as one to be finally reached, but one to enjoy along the way.

And yet such a child cannot aim at less than his entire approval. He will not abuse such a comfort or count it the chief thing; but ever seeing more fully the vast importance of all his Father's interests, and his earnest desire to make him a workman that needeth not to be ashamed, he will ever beseech Him not to spare his correction, but to show him faithfully every fault, that it may be rectified, and that he may be "made meet to be partaker of the inheritance of the saints in light."

(4) EXPLANATION.

Sanctification is distinguished from justification, thus: Justification changes our state in law, before God as a Judge. Sanctification changes our heart and life, before Him as our Father. Justification precedes, and sanctification commonly commences and follows, in proportion as the converted man strives, by faith, to grow in grace, as the fruit and evidence of the new life in the soul. Justification removes the penalty of sin. Sanctification restrains the power of temptation to sin, while undiminished faith in the aid of Christ, remains in full exercise, like that of Peter in walking on the water. Whenever his faith intermitted, in the slightest degree, he sank beneath the waves. So it must be with the sanctified Christian. If faith intermits, he will fall into sin. Justification delivers us from the avenging wrath of God. Sanctification conforms us to His image more and more. In a theological sense, justification means remission of deserved penalty for sin,—an act of free grace, by which God pardons a sinner, and accepts him as righteous, on account of the atonement of Christ. And faith is that voluntary trust in the atoning death of Christ, by which a sinner who cannot be justified by personal excellencies or good works, is treated by God as though he were just. Justification not only delivers from punishment, but bestows positive favor, in treating men on the first act of genuine faith as though they were perfectly holy. " The blood of Christ cleanseth from all sin." And this adoption is immediately connected with justification. (*a*) Adoption is simply a new and specific species of justification. (*b*) It is an intense description. By adoption the justified children of God become heirs of God and joint heirs with Christ. But entire sanctification as a state, in an evangelical sense, is the act of God's grace by which the affections of men are purified or alienated from sin and the world, and exalted to such a supreme love to God as shall ensure continuous obedience to the divine law from the best of intentions. This is the meaning in the passages, " The very God of peace sanctify you wholly ; " " Sanctify them through Thy truth ; " "Through sanctification of the Spirit." Although there is a clear distinction between justification and sanctification, they are inseparably connected in the promises of God. " For whom He justifies He also sanctifies, and whom He sanctifies He also glorifies." " Ye are washed, ye are sanctified, ye are justified, in the name of the Lord Jesus, and by the Spirit of our God."

I. In what respects do justified and sanctified Christians agree ? (*a*) It seems plain, according to the Scriptures, that both the justified and the sanctified begin the Christian life with entire consecration as the unalterable condition of Christian discipleship.

For the Great Teacher has said, " Thou shalt love the Lord thy God with all thy heart,"—which does not mean a part of it. " What does the Lord thy God require of thee, but to do justly and to love mercy, and to walk humbly with thy God." " Ye shall seek Me, and find Me, when ye shall search for Me with all your heart." There is no promise of finding God with partial consecration. And with such supreme love to God and devotion to His service in regeneration, the sinner changes his controlling purpose from sin to holiness. There can be no partial consecration, no compromise between serving God and serving the world. " Ye cannot serve God and Mammon." " Whosoever he be of you that forsaketh not all that he hath, he cannot be my disciple." Did not Peter say to Ananias, who made a partial consecration, " Why hath satan filled thy heart, to lie to the Holy Ghost, to keep back part of the price?" What does God say is the difference between the regenerate and the unregenerate? " When ye were the servants of sin, ye were free from righteousness, but now being made free from sin, and become the servants of God, ye have your fruit unto holiness." (*b*) Both these classes are alike in the fact of their justification. " Being justified freely by His grace, through the redemption that is in Christ Jesus." " Being justified by faith, we have peace with God, through our Lord Jesus Christ." " For with the heart man believeth unto righteousness." And the moment the sinner heartily complies with these terms he is an accepted candidate for heaven. " If we confess our sins, God is faithful and just to forgive us our sins and cleanse us from all unrighteousness." (c) Both the justified and the sanctified are exposed to temptation. They are tempted by the world, the flesh and the devil. Sometimes they are tempted to neglect duty, sometimes directly and positively to transgress the divine law. Even those who have made the highest practical attainments in sanctification, perhaps even greater than the merely justified, have struggles with spiritual enemies peculiar to an advanced state of grace. For so it seems to have been with Jesus. "For we have not a High Priest, which cannot be touched with the feelings of our infirmities, but was in all points tempted like as we are, yet without sin." "The disciple is not above his Master, nor the servant above his Lord." "It is enough for the disciple that he be as his Master." "Blessed is the man that endureth temptation." (d) Both the justified and sanctified, as free agents, are liable to yield to temptation and fall into sin. If a holy angel could fall and become a devil, if a holy Adam was not free from the liability of sinning, it is certainly possible with the holiest of Christians.

II. Points of difference between justified and sanctified Christians. (a) Those who are merely justified, and repeatedly fall under the power of temptation, find their experience delineated in Romans, seventh chapter, from the fourteenth to the twenty-fourth verse. While the sanctified Christian finds his experience delineated in the sixth chapter, from the first to the eleventh verse, and the eighth chapter, from the first to the fourth verse, inclusive, and from the thirty-fifth to the thirty-ninth verse, inclusive. (*b*) Those who are habitually in a state of sanctification, grow in grace more rapidly than those who live in a mere state of justification. Growth in grace consists in the increasing strength of holy affections, and consequent frequency of holy volitions. Those who are merely justified, so frequently yield to temptation, that their progress in the divine life is greatly impeded. When they yield to inordinate desire, darkness settles down upon their souls and hinders their progress. They feel condemned. They flounder in the bitterness of penitence until by a new and voluntary act of faith, they cast themselves on the Saviour and obtain peace in believing. And in the midst of their back-sliding and discouragement, they cry out: " The law is holy and the commandment holy. But sin, that it might appear sin, worketh death in me by that which is good; that sin by the commandment might become exceeding sinful. For we know that the law is spiritual, but I am carnal, sold under sin. For that which I do I allow not, for what I would, that do I not; but what I hate, that do I. O wretched man that I am! Who shall deliver me from the body of this death?' But those who commonly, if not uniformly, live in a state of sanctification, by continuous and more frequent victories over temptation through faith in Christ's promised assistance, accelerate their progress in piety. In proportion to their continuous victories, their love, their gratitude, their faith, their penitence—their humility increases, while the power of temptation gradually and naturally weakens in its assaults upon them.

Thus all their increasing power of love and devoted service will strengthen their affections and holy purposes of faithful obedience, while in proportion as they resist the devil will he flee from them, and the fascinations of the world and the flesh will lose their enchanting power to enslave their free spirits. By a better improvement of the means of grace, by searching the Scriptures, and more intimate communion with God, sanctified Christians will follow more strictly the example of Jesus, who was holy, harmless, undefiled, separate from sinners, who increased in favor with God and man. The faultless Saviour grew in grace. And we know, on the principles of analogy, that we too may grow in grace more rapidly in proportion as we become assimilated to him. For we know that our love for a friend worthy of our love, increases more rapidly in proportion as we enjoy his society and meditate upon his superior excellencies. And in our relation to our Divine Master, we are taught that "the path of the just is as the shining light which shineth more and more unto the perfect day." Thus we perceive that the entirely sanctified differ widely from the merely justified, in this kind of experience. They are commonly, as the rule and purpose of life, victorious over temptation. Thus their souls are saved from darkness, discouragement, bitterness and anguish. Sometimes their souls suffer through manifold temptations. But they stand and triumph, gaining repeated victories, through faith in Christ's proffered assistance. Thus, unhindered by voluntary neglect of duty or positive transgression, sanctified souls can say from blessed experience, "We all with open face beholding, as in a glass, the glory of the Lord, are changed into the same image, from glory to glory, even as by the spirit of the Lord." And says the inspired apostle, "reckon ye also yourselves to be dead indeed unto sin, but alive unto God through Jesus Christ our Lord." "For sin shall not have dominion over you, for ye are not under the law but under grace." "But, God be thanked, that ye were the servants of sin; but ye have obeyed from the heart that form of doctrine which was delivered you." (c) "'The sanctified soul," as a writer has observed, "has received the fulfillment of the new covenant, while the merely justified has not. In the Old Testament times, God declared to the people through the prophets, that the days were coming when He should make a new covenant with His church. 'This shall be the covenant that I shall make with the House of Israel,' saith the Lord. 'I will put my law into their inward parts and write it in their hearts. Then will I sprinkle clean water upon you, and ye shall be clean; from all your filthiness and from all your idols will I cleanse you; a new heart also will I give you, and a new spirit will I put within you; and 1 will take away the stony heart out of your flesh, and I will give you a heart of flesh; and I will put my Spirit within you, and cause you to walk in My statutes; and ye shall keep My judgments and do them. In that day there shall be a fountain opened to the House of David, and to the inhabitants of Jerusalem, for sin and for uncleanness. In those days, and at that time,' saith the Lord, 'the iniquity of Israel shall be sought for, and there shall be none, and the sins of Judah, and they shall not be found.' This is God's new covenant. It became due to the Church at the death of Christ. One of the objects of the epistle to the Hebrews is to explain this covenant, and urge it upon their acceptance. Under this covenant the Church lives to day. In this covenant, the present privileges of the Church are laid down. The Apostolic Church claimed and received its fulfillment. Some individuals have, since then. Spiritual power and holiness have marked these persons. The covenant is to sanctify wholly every believing soul, and sustain it in this state blameless the remainder of this life, and forever in heaven. This is 'the promise of eternal life.' The sanctified soul has received in itself the fulfillment of the promise; and has already entered upon its 'eternal inheritance of righteousness, peace and joy in the Holy Ghost.'" This is not true of the soul simply justified. This soul has not yet availed itself of God's provisions for its sanctification. It has felt its need of the grace of pardon and acceptance. It has sought this by coming into the spirit of obedience, and has obtained it. Now, it must feel its need of sanctifying grace, and must ask in faith, holding on until it receives, and its joy is full. The sanctified soul has received the fulfillment of the new covenant; the soul simply justified has not. The sanctified soul maintains a conscience void of offence toward God and man; while a soul simply justified does not. Justification brings the soul into a state of good conscience. It meets all present obligations. Conscience approves so long as the soul is in this state, and condemns not. But to its distress, the justified soul finds itself frequently sinning. Then approval of conscience gives way to condemnation. As a judge it passes sentence; as an internal executioner it inflicts punishment. The soul writhes in pain. David brings out many of these experiences in the Psalms. The simply justified soul does not continuously maintain a conscience " void of offence toward God and toward man." Indulged sin and neglected duty bring frequent sorrow. Not only does this soul more or less commit sin, but it comes into fearfulness that it shall. The future is often filled with forebodings. Convinced of its weakness, but not having appropriated Christ's strength, anxiety rests heavily upon it. Thus it is led to seek and find full salvation. The sanctified soul has not this present experience. This is a thing of the past. A good conscience is maintained; no wilful neglect of duty takes place. Temptation is not yielded to; the soul overcomes. It can truly say: " I live with all good conscience."—" The law of the Spirit of life in Christ Jesus, hath made me free from the law of sin and death." By mighty reigning grace it is kept in this state. It is not condemned. In the soul is peace; Christ is the source of its love: By grace He has begotten it; by grace he sustains it. The flowing righteousness of the soul emanates from Christ. Its righteousness is produced by the grace of Christ. In this sense Christ is its righteousness. It gives Christ all the glory. (*d*) " The sanctified soul has such strength of love as to secure its resistance to all temptation, and its performance of all duty; this is not true of a soul simply justified. The soul sanctified is delivered. The law of the spirit of life in Christ Jesus is its Deliverer. The influences of the life-giving Spirit induce that strength of love which overcomes." "Herein is our love made perfect." In the sanctified soul a higher form of love exists. Choice is stronger, emotions are deeper and more easily aroused; the sensibility is quickened—its emotiveness is heightened; views of the infinite value of Christ's honor and glory far surpass those of a simply justified person. So also, do those appreciate the infinite worth of souls. Choice is energized—there is power in it; it struggles unconquerably to promote its end. God must be glorified. Man must be saved and blessed. "Self must be left out of the question," says the sanctified soul. Here is realization of truth, with invincibleness of choice, and depth and quickness of feeling, emotive love. The soul says to temptation: "Stand thou there, I am God's. I have something else to do than to violate law, order, conscience, reason and truth in the gratification of self. I have a God to glorify. The eternal interests of souls hang on my influence and efforts."

> "Away! vain, vile tempters, away!
> Perishing things of clay,
> Born but for one brief day.
> Tempt not my soul away."

This is the attitude of the sanctified soul toward temptation, either to forms of sin or neglect of duty. There is a strength of love produced and sustained by the Holy Spirit, which bids defiance to all temptation, and which leads the soul, simply trusting Christ for strength, to fearlessly close in at once, with all duty and in all things to triumph in God. The weak love of a simply justified soul, more or less gives way to temptation, and often sings its own peculiar lamentation:—

"Prone to wander, Lord, I feel it.
Prone to leave the God I love."

(e) The sanctified soul has fellowship with the Father and His Son, Jesus Christ, which the merely justified soul has not. This is one of the highest forms of Christian experience. It can be understood by none but those who have it. It may be desired however by all. It may be possessed by all who will in faith seek it of God. The convert or justified person has this experience in a faint degree. In this "fellowship" are several elements and several high degrees of blessedness. There is the element of sensible companionship. Many converted persons feel that Christ is further from them than are the stars. They gaze about, above. They see no Jesus, they realize none. Jesus seems withdrawn from the universe. Especially do souls feel thus, if at conversion they had some light and realization of Christ's love. These feelings have gone away. Darkness has settled in. There was no need of this. But it is a fact, resulting from want of instruction, or unwatchfulness. They feel alone. Where is Jesus? Oh, they don't know! They feel like ascending up to heaven, or descending into the deep to find Him. They do not realize His presence. He seems far away. In a wicked, unfriendly world they feel alone. O, the loneliness of such loneliness! The soul breaks forth with Job: "O, that I knew where I might find Him!" This is not the experience of a back-slider, but of a soul being drawn by the Holy Spirit, to feel its need of sensible union with Christ, and to desire it deeply. It does not want Christ to seem like a star in the distant firmament. It wants "a God at hand and not afar off." This experience characterizes persons not made perfect in love in this sense; sometimes they have seasons of joyful nearness to Christ, but these are exceptions. A sense of His absence is the general rule; a sense of His presence, the exception. With a sanctified soul, the opposite is true. A sense of Christ's absence is the exception. A sense of His presence is the general rule. The soul feels Christ is with it. When it thinks of Him He seem near. He dwells within. The soul knows it from the experience which it has of divine comforts and illuminations. When illumination is temporarily withdrawn, it trusts Him. It feels perfectly safe. A faithful Saviour is pledged to keep it. Thus with shadow and shining, as the blessed Jesus sees best, the soul realizes the truth—more and more—" Lo; I am with you." (*f*) Another element of fellowship is divine union. A sympathy of the human soul with the divine. The soul justified generally laments a disinclination to meditate closely on religious truth. The mind does not seem to run on this so easily as it does on secular subjects. It also mourns a want of feeling; also a disposition to have its own will, and not Christ's. In the sanctified soul the mind naturally runs on religion. This is its joyful meditation every moment possible. It has feeling enough; so there is and can be no condemnation on this point. Then it has a sweet consciousness that its own will is blended wholly with Christ's. His will is its will, even to the loss of all earthly comforts, and of life itself. This is the continual state of a soul entirely sanctified. As the soul grows in grace many other blessed experiences develop themselves, so that we all, "beholding as in a glass, the glory of the Lord, are changed from glory into glory," by the power of the Holy Spirit. (*g*) The sanctified soul has Christ actually so revealed to it from time to time, that all its wants are met. The soul simply justified, mourns over wants unsupplied. One soul realizes the blessedness of the truth: "Ye are complete in Him." The other has not learned to avail itself of completeness in Christ. If it trusted Christ, if its faith did not fail, all needed grace would momentarily be given. But when the time comes to walk on the water, faith too often fails, and the soul sinks, crying, "Lord save me,"—to rise again. The faith of the sanctified soul does not fail; hence, constant grace and constant supply for all real soul-wants. (*h*) The sanctified soul trusts Christ as sanctifier, as well as justifier; the simply justified soul does not. It has not yet learned to do this. Perhaps it has not yet felt much need of sanctification, or the gift of such grace, as will rectify the sensibility and establish the soul in love. Perhaps feeling its need, it has been taught the devil's greatest lie, that this grace is not attainable in this life—that Christ will entirely sanctify the soul in this life, and preserve it in this state, if he is trusted as taught in I. Thess. v : 23-24. Perhaps, hungering and thirsting, it has not received any practical teaching on this subject, and is groping in doubt and darkness. At any rate it does not trust Christ as its entire sanctifier, as it does as its justifier. But the sanctified soul does this. It as much trusts Christ, to keep it sanctified as justified. And it finds Him as faithful in one of those offices as in the other.

> Blessed Jesus, I would be
> Perfectly conformed to Thee;
> Washed in Thine own precious blood,
> Wholly sanctified to God.
> Thou alone hast power, I know,
> Full salvation to bestow;
> And I trust Thy gracious will,
> This petition to fulfil.
>
> Blessed Jesus! even now,
> While before Thy cross I bow,
> Let the crimson, cleansing tide,
> Flowing from Thy opened side,
> Through my heart its passage take
> Me a holy temple make—
> Where Thy will, and Thine alone,
> Shall forever have its throne.
>
> Blessed Jesus, Thou dost hear!
> " Perfect love casts out all fear."
> While Thy promise I believe,
> Full salvation I receive.
> Oh, the bliss, the joy, the peace!
> I from sin have sweet release.
> Blessed Jesus! unto Thee,
> Evermore the praise shall be.

### (5) NOT SELF-RIGHTEOUS.

Being truly sanctified, such Christians are free from self-sufficiency and self-righteousness and deeply feel the need of God's supporting grace to enable them to resist temptation. They feel the need of the Holy Spirit's constant guidance, lest by their ignorance or neglect of constant watchfulness, they fall into grievous mistakes or be tempted to indulge in known or wilful sins.

### (6) NOT BOASTFUL OF ATTAINMENTS.

Knowing their fallibility and liability to mistake in judging of the moral character of their intentions and volitions for a single day, those who entertain intelligent and truly humble views of themselves join with Job in his confession, "If I justify myself, mine own mouth shall condemn me, if I say I am perfect, (that is faultless), it shall also prove me perverse."

### (7) CRITICISMS OF MEN UNREASONABLE.

But at the same time with an enlightened moral judgment, "having a good conscience," they may feel assured that their loving service is acceptable and approved of God, while their outward conduct may fail to meet, or satisfy the unreasonable demands and criticisms of men, who look for divine infallibility or absolute, or angelic faultlessness. Their honest and faithful intention to serve God according to the best of their ability at all times, can be known only to themselves and the "Searcher of hearts." "For the Lord seeth not as man seeth, for man looketh on the outward appearance, but the Lord looketh on the heart." But in proportion to their absolute holiness sanctified Christians (if they humbly profess it) must expect to encounter the severest criticisms. For it was said of John, the beloved disciple, " he hath a devil," and of the Son of man who did no sin, " behold a man gluttonous and a wine bibber." In judging of justified or sanctified Christians, critics should notice the best and not the poorest specimens.

(8) TEMPTATIONS NOT SINFUL.

But in order to render entire sanctification in this life possible, or to render it possible for any finite, depraved man, through the operations of the Holy Ghost, and implicit faith in the victorious power and aid of Jesus Christ, to cease from sin at all, it must be understood, that neither native proneness to sin, nor outward temptation to sin, are not themselves actually sinful. Temptation is the necessary test of character. If a man is not tempted he cannot prove the strength of his capacity for resistance. There can be no evidence of his obedience or his practical holiness.

(9) DISTINCTION BETWEEN DEPRAVITY AND SIN, OR PHYSICAL AND MORAL DEPRAVITY.

(EXTRACT.)

Depravity always implies a departure from a state of original integrity, or from conformity to the laws of the being who is the subject of depravity, whether these laws be physical or moral. Physical depravity is the depravity of constitution, or substance, of the body or mind. Physical depravity, when predicated of the body, is commonly and rightly termed disease. When physical depravity is predicated of mind, it is intended that the powers of the mind either in substance or in consequence of their connection with and dependence upon the body, are in a diseased, degenerate state, so that the healthy action of those powers is not sustained. But physical depravity, whether of body or mind, can have no moral character in itself, for the plain reason that it is involuntary, and in its nature disease and not sin. Physical depravity can be predicated of any organized substance. It is a possible state of every organized substance or being in existence. As mind in connection with body, manifests itself through it, acts by means of it, and is dependent upon it, it is plain that if the body becomes diseased, or physically depraved, the mind cannot but be affected by this state of the body, through and by means of which it acts. The normal manifestations of mind cannot, in such cases, be reasonably expected. Physical depravity may be predicated of all the powers and involuntary states of the mind, of the intelligence, of the sensibility, and of the faculty of the will. That is, the actings and states of the intelligence may become disordered, depraved, deranged, or fallen from the state of integrity and healthiness. In this way the sensibility, or feeling department of the mind, may be sadly and physically depraved. The appetites and passions, the desires and cravings, the antipathies and repellencies of the feelings, fall into great disorder and anarchy. Numerous artificial appetites are generated, and the whole sensibility becomes a chaos of conflicting and clamorous desires, emotions and passions. And this condition is commonly owing to the state of the nervous system with which it is connected, through and by which it manifests itself. Thus it appears that the human body is in a state of physical depravity, and the human mind also manifests human depravity. But such hereditary depravity as this, transmitted from Adam as well as from our immediate parentage with no voluntary choice of our own, can have no moral character in our earliest infancy, or be absolutely sinful, however much it may predispose us to the commission of sin. For we cannot rationally believe that Adam made his posterity sinners, by transferring to them the guilt of his first transgression. "Guilt is a personal thing, which belongs to him alone who does a sinful action." The guilt of any action can no more be transferred from the agent to another person, than the action itself. Adam could not transfer his first act of disobedience to his posterity; and if he could not transfer the act itself, it is equally evident that he could not transfer the guilt of it. As he could not have made himself guilty of eating of the forbidden fruit without choosing to eat of it, so he could not make his posterity guilty of eating of the forbidden fruit without their choosing to do the same action. But we know that he never made them choose to commit his first sin; and therefore he could not bring them under the guilt of his first transgression. It was as much out of the power of Adam to transfer his own personal guilt to his posterity, as it is now out of the power of any other parent to transfer his own personal guilt to his children. It seems obvious that even the Supreme Being, in His righteous sovereignty, could not consistently transfer the guilt of Adam's sin to his posterity. And no constitution which He could make could render such a mode of conduct consistent with His moral rectitude. Shall not the Judge of All the Earth do right? Shall He, therefore, transfer the guilt of the father to the son? or shall He punish the son for the father's sin? No! "The soul that sinneth, it shall die," for its own iniquity. But here I observe that moral depravity is essentially distinct from physical depravity. It is synonymous with real sinfulness. And sin we know is any want of conformity to, or transgression of, the divine law. Moral depravity is the depravity of free will, not of the faculty itself, but of its free action. It consists in a violation of the moral law. Depravity of the will, as a faculty, is or would be physical, and not moral depravity. It would be depravity of substance and not of free responsible choice. Moral depravity is depravity of choice. It is a choice at variance with moral law, moral right. It is moral depravity because it consists in a violation of moral law, and because it has moral character. Hence, moral depravity, or sin, consists in sinning, and nothing else. It consists in free, voluntary violations of moral law, for moral law legislates only over free, intelligent choices. There is, therefore, no morally corrupt nature, distinct from free, voluntary, sinful exercises. Adam had no such nature, and therefore could convey no such nature to his posterity. But even supposing that he really had a morally corrupt nature, distinct from his free, voluntary sinful exercises, it must have belonged to his soul and not to his body. And if it belonged to his soul he could not convey it to his posterity, who derive their soul's immediately from the fountain of being. God is the father of our spirits. The soul is not transmitted from father to son by natural generation. The soul is spiritual, and what is spiritual is indivisible; and what is indivisible is incapable of propagation. Now if with such plain statements and facts in mind, showing the essential difference between depravity and sin, or physical and moral depravity, any person shall still believe in constitutional and native sinfulness of the substance of the human soul before its voluntary wrong choices, it is not reasonable to expect that he ever will be a believer in the highest practical piety, or in entire consecration, or in perfectly acceptable obedience to the divine law for an hour, or a day, or a month. Nor in the statement "If there be first a willing mind, it is accepted according to that a man hath, and not according to that he hath not."

(10) SIN VOLUNTARY.

The voluntary indulgence of vicious thoughts or a voluntary choice to do wrong, or voluntary neglect to do right, only can be sinful, as all actual sin must be voluntary. For all sin comprehensively expressed, is any want of conformity unto or transgression of the law of God. Such is the teaching of God himself. "All have sinned, and come short of the glory of God." "Sin is the transgression of the law." "For if there be first a willing mind, it is accepted according to that a man hath, and not according to that he hath not."

### (11) MISTAKES NOT SINFUL.

And it must be understood that mistakes which may occur in connection with the most fair-minded and industrious pursuit of all accessible light in favor of the right and of duty, cannot he properly considered as positively sinful.

### (12) INTENTION.

It is the wrong motive and evil intention which constitute the essential wickedness of any mental determination or outward act. A truly benevolent and conscientious intention cannot be sinful in the sight of the "Searcher of hearts." "For as a man thinketh in his heart so is he." The Christian's intention to please his Heavenly Father renders his moral acts holy. And a right and benevolent intention must control the whole life so that he may be free from sin. For it is obvious that an obedient intention renders an act holy in the sight of God. It is the test of its moral character. Says President Wayland, "In a deliberate action four distinct elements may be commonly observed. These are:

First—The outward act, as when I put money into the hands of another.

Second—The conception of this act, of which the external performance is the mere bodying forth.

Third—The resolution to carry that conception into effect.

Fourth—The intention or design with which all this is done.

Now the moral quality does not belong to the external act; for the same external act may be performed by two men, while its moral character is, in the two cases entirely dissimilar. Nor does it belong to the conception of the act, nor to the resolution to carry that conception into effect, for the resolution to perform an action can have no other character than that of the action itself. It must, then, reside in the intention. That such is the fact may be illustrated by an example: A. and B. both give to C. a piece of money. They both conceived of this action before they performed it They both resolved to do precisely what they did. In all this both actions coincide. A. however gave it to C. with the intention of procuring the murder of a friend; B. with the intention of relieving a family in distress. It is evident that in this case, the intention gives to the action its character, as right and wrong. By reference to the intention, we inculpate or exculpate others, or ourselves, without any respect to the happiness or misery actually produced. Let the result of an action be what it may, we hold a man guilty, simply on the ground of intention, or on the same ground we hold him innocent. Thus also of ourselves. We are conscious of guilt or innocence, not from the result of an action, but from the intention by which we were actuated." " For as a man thinketh in his heart, so is he." This is the moral test of his actions. Therefore, "keep thy heart with all diligence, for out of it are the issues of life." And the supreme ultimate motive determines the moral act to be absolutely holy or sinful."

### (13) MORAL ACTIONS SIMPLE—NOT MIXED.

(ABSTRACT.)

In order that a man may cease from voluntarily sinning for a moment, or a day, the simplicity of the nature of every specific volition must be admitted. That each action involving moral character, must be perfectly holy or perfectly sinful. Right action is impartial benevolent action, including our own welfare, according to its value in our relations both to God and our fellow-men. Wrong action is unreasonable, selfish action, involving a disregard for the authority and claims of God and the reasonable and just rights of our race. Therefore a sinner, in order to be a Christian, must totally abandon his native selfishness, and choose to seek supremely the general good. Hence it is obvious that these opposite choices of supreme selfishness and supreme benevolence, cannot co-exist and be operative in the same person at the same time in the same sense. "The co-existence of sin and holiness, or of two opposite moral states, is impossible." " No man can serve two masters: for either he will hate the one and love the other, or else he will hold to the one and despise the other. Ye cannot serve God and mammon." By this is not meant that no man can serve two masters at different times. For Adam, once the servant of God, became a sinner, and for aught we know repented, and again became the servant of God. But two opposite intentions, both to serve God and disobey Him, cannot co-exist. Therefore it is impossible for a moral action to be mixed as the product of two opposing motives, both good and bad. " Whosoever shall keep the whole law, and yet offend in one point, he is guilty of all." Offending in one point, is breaking one moral precept. What is the ground of the assertion, that this is breaking the whole law? This, manifestly: "The law is a unity, the one impartial demand of reason—however multiform in its expression, however varied in its application. The will is an integral unit, one and all in every intention." It must then be wholly co-incident with reason's law, or wholly discordant with it, whatever particular precept or practical application of the law it may transgress or obey. But it may be objected that when a Christian sins, if the doctrine of the simplicity of moral actions be true, he becomes as bad as he was before his conversion, and worse if possible, having sinned against more light. He therefore as much needs a second conversion as he did the first, and this we should think would be less likely to take place. To this objection it may be replied that a Christian is one who knows by experience the love of God, the blessedness of an approving conscience, and the consolation of the Christian's hope; and when he sins will be in a condition very different from that of one who has never experienced these things, though during the time of his transgression he may be equally, or if you please, more guilty.

Therefore the sin of the Christian involves no less guilt than that of impenitent sinners, who have never been converted, but its abandonment is more sure, or if you please, it is certain.

But it may be said if the simplicity of moral actions be true, a man might be a Christian and a sinner alternately several times a day. But by this objection it is merely said that a man might sin and repent several times a day. This is doubtless true. For continued obedience is certainly not a necessity but an imperative duty and a most precious privilege through faith in Christ.

In moral philosophy we read that " moral obligation, merit, demerit, &c., pertain immediately to acts of will, or voluntary states of mind only. No state of the physical organization, nor of the intelligence, or sensibility can, with any truth or propriety, be denominated a moral action. Of acts of will, ultimate intentions only possess a moral character, or can properly be denominated moral actions. The question before us then is legitimately reduced to this one single inquiry, namely: can any one given ultimate intention be of a mixed moral character; in other words, can such distinct, contradictory and opposite elements as sin and holiness, selfishness and benevolence, voluntary obedience and disobedience to known duty, enter into one and the same ultimate act of will, or intention? Can contradictory and opposite elements enter into one and the same ultimate intention? To this question I answer, no; for the following reasons :

(*a*) The dogma of mixed moral action, in the sense

now under consideration, is in palpable contradiction to all our fundamental conceptions of an ultimate intention. Such intention implies not only the election of its object for its own sake, but a corresponding rejection of everything of an opposite nature. Suppose the question is before my mind, shall I go to this place or that? I can by no possibility go to but one of the places named, and to one or the other I must go. Now a determination to go to one place implies of necessity a determination not to go to the other. The same does and must hold true in respect to all ultimate intentions. The question before the mind is; shall I, for example, serve God or mammon? A determination to serve one implies and necessarily involves a corresponding determination not to serve the other; the demands of each being directly opposite and contradictory to the other. An ultimate intention then embracing the contradictory and opposite elements of voluntary obedience and disobedience, would imply, in one and the same act, a determination to serve and not to serve God, and a determination not to serve and actually to serve mammon. This is a palpable absurdity, as great as the supposition that the same body may move in opposite directions at one and the same time. So Edwards himself affirms. "It is absurd," he says, "to suppose the same individual will to oppose itself in its present act; or the present choice to be opposite to and resisting present choice; as absurd as it is to talk of two contrary motions in the same moving body at the same time."

(*b*) An intention, to be ultimate, must be supreme,

that is, it must involve the supreme preference of the mind. The supposition of two distinct and ultimate intentions in the mind at one and the same time, or of one involving the contradictory elements under consideration, which would in fact be equivalent to two, implies of necessity that neither is supreme, that is, that neither or both together are in reality an ultimate intention. The idea of two such intentions, then, or of two contradictory elements in one and the same intention, implies a palpable contradiction and impossibility. "Christ denies," says Calvin, "that it can be that any one should obey God and his flesh at one and the same time." " The supreme affections," says Mr. Barnes, "can be fixed on only one object. 'So,' says Jesus, ' the servant of God cannot at the same time obey Him and be avaricious, or seek treasures supremely on earth.' "

(c) Nor is inspiration silent on such a point. Take a single passage in illustration: "Whosoever keepeth the whole law, and yet offendeth in one point, he is guilty of all." The obvious meaning of this passage is this: If all the particular volitions or external acts of an individual are in harmony with the law of God, with one exception, that only being in opposition to it, this demonstrates the fact, that the entire ultimate intention of the agent from which the whole series proceeds is in opposition to the law, and consequently, that the whole moral state of the individual is sinful and totally so. No meaning attaches to this passage if this is not it. The same doctrine is manifestly affirmed by our Saviour in the assertion; "Whosoever cometh after me and forsaketh not all that he hath, he cannot be my disciple." The obvious meaning of the passage is, that until all particular acts are in full harmony with the known will of Christ, no ultimate intention, such as is requisite to discipleship, that is, no intention morally right, can possibly exist.

The dogma under consideration is alike opposed to the positive teachings of reason and revelation both. The following are the conclusions necessarily resulting from the doctrine above established. When all the voluntary acts and states of a moral agent are in all respects what they are required to be, he stands perfect and complete in his obedience to the moral law, as far as present duty is concerned. No blame attaches to him for any states of the physical system or intelligence, or sensibility, unavoidably co-existing with voluntary obedience to the universal voice of duty. No moral agent is at any moment virtuous at all, whose voluntary acts and states are not for the time being in full harmony with all known duty, in other words, with all forms of obligation really then resting upon him. There is no avoiding this conclusion.

(14) IF PERFECT KNOWLEDGE IS NECESSARY, ENTIRE SANCTIFICATION IS IMPOSSIBLE.

If therefore, in order to be sanctified wholly, and cease from sin for a single day, a short-sighted and finite being must be infallible in his moral judgment, and such an experience must be forever impossible on earth, or in the perfect society and holiness of heaven.

### (15) DIVINE PRESERVATION.

Now in order that God may preserve the justified Christian from falling into final condemnation, "he must believe with the heart unto righteousness." And in order that the sanctified Christian may be preserved from yielding to the power of temptation for a day, or year, or series of years, he must continually trust in God's proffered grace "to keep him in all his ways," so that it may become more and more the prevailing habit of his whole life to live constantly in a state, not only of entire, but continuous sanctification. And if through any neglect of watchfulness against the sudden and unanticipated assaults of special temptation, and the intermission of his strength of faith in Christ's interposition and aid, he should be momentarily overcome by the adversary, he will instantly repent, so that sin shall be the exception and not, as is too frequently the case, the prevailing rule of life.

### (16) ABILITY COMMENSURATE WITH OBLIGATION.

The truly sanctified Christian must love and obey God continually, with all his present powers of body and mind. " For if there be first a willing mind, it is accepted according to that a man hath, and not according to that he hath not."

As Mr. Barnes, the commentator, very sensibly observes, " If the heart is in it, then the offering will be acceptable to God, whether you be able to give much or little. A willing mind is the first consideration. In such a case God will approve of the gift, and will receive it favorably. A man is not required to give what he has not. His obligation is proportioned to his ability. The great and obviously just and equal principle stated in the verse here quoted, was originally applied by Paul, to the duty of giving alms. But it is equally true and just as applied to all the duties which we owe to God. He demands first, a willing mind, a heart disposed to yield obedience. He claims that our service should be voluntary and sincere, and that we should make an unreserved consecration of what we have. Secondly, he demands only what we have power to render. He requires a service strictly according to our ability, and to be measured by that. He demands no more than our powers are fitted to produce; no more than we are able to render. Our obligations in all cases are limited by our ability. This is obviously the rule of equity, and this is all that is anywhere demanded in the Bible—and this is everywhere demanded. Thus our love to Him is to be in proportion to our ability, and not to be graduated by the ability of angels or other beings. 'And thou shalt love the Lord thy God with all thy heart, and with all thy soul, and with all thy mind, and with all thy strength.' The love is to be commensurate with ability. So of repentence, faith, and obedience, in any form. None but a tyrant ever demands more than can be rendered, and to demand more is the appropriate description of a tyrant, and cannot pertain to the ever blessed God. Therefore, 'if any man minister let him do it as of the ability which God giveth.' No one is bound to go beyond this ability, every one is required to come up to it."

### (17) REQUIREMENT OF THE LAW.

"Love is the fulfilling of the law." And this law requires the truly sanctified Christian to abstain entirely from everything which he knows to be wrong in thought, word or deed. And as the Holy Spirit and divine truth are the means used in sanctification, he must heartily believe the truth, and in the power and willingness of Jesus to give him the victory over temptation, and surrender his whole being to the Holy Spirit, to be continuously moulded into the very image of his Divine Master. His will must be in constant subjection to God's will, not willing what he knows to be wrong, or contrary to Bible truth. In cases of doubt about the divine will, he must not and will not follow his own natural inclinations, but promptly obey the will of Jesus, in proportion as duty may be revealed to him, in God's word or providence.

### (18) SANCTIFIED AFFLICTIONS.

Even in afflictions he must be entirely and cheerfully submissive; "for the Lord our God is righteous in all His works which He doeth." And we know that all things work together for good to them that love God, to them who are called according to His purpose." Therefore the submissive Christian says to God, "not as I will, but as Thou wilt."

> "What if poor sinners count my grief,
> The sign of an unchastened will,
> He who can give my soul relief,
> Knows that I'm submissive still.
> Henceforth my own desire shall be,

> That He who knows the best should choose for me;
> And so, whate'er His love sees good to send,
> I'll trust its best, because He knows the end."

"Behold, I have refined thee," says God, "but not with silver. I have chosen thee in the furnace of affliction." In such experiences the growing Christian is more desirous that his afflictions should have a sanctifying influence on him than that they should be removed. Such a Christian is submissive, and hopes in the darkest afflictions. "And every man that hath this hope in him purifieth himself even as He is pure." He opens the shutters of the dark chambers of his soul and lets in the three ineffable rays of the sun of righteousness with healing in his wings; God's perfect love, knowledge and power. He knows that the heavens will fall, before, with such attributes, He can harm a hair of His children's heads. These three rays together, form this blessed pencil of light. "He hath done all things well."

> "To have each day the things I wish,
> Lord, seemeth best to me!
> But not to have some things I wish,
> Lord seemeth best to Thee.
> Henceforth then let 'thy will be done,'
> Though mine, O God, be crossed;
> Myself in Thee all lost!"

(19) ERRORS TO BE AVOIDED.

(ABSTRACT.)

"Before entering upon the direct proof of the attainability of entire sanctification in this life, it seems expedient to guard seekers against some common mistakes. It is probable that all intelligent Christians believe, as a writer of experience has observed, in the following extracts: "That the possibilities of Christian attainment rise continually higher and higher, above any supposable point he may have reached, so long as his mental faculties retain their normal activity, and he has God's word before him. God's providences all round about him, and God's spirit within him, there will be yet Alps on Alps rising ever before, up which he may be continually ascending;" but the common term, higher life, seems to involve some mistakes which should be avoided.

It is maintained that the "lower life" begins with a first conversion, the higher with a second conversion, analogous to the first, yet quite unlike it. The lower commences with regeneration; the higher with a special form and peculiar measure of sanctification. The lower begins with faith in Christ for pardon; the higher makes utmost account of its own commencing act of "faith for the blessing" of a cleansed heart. Such ideas seem in some measure erroneous. The Scriptures clearly teach what Christain attainment is, and its possibilities in the present life.

A new creation; old things are passed away; all things become new, the promise fulfilled. "I will put My spirit within you, and cause you to walk in My statutes," "abiding in Christ," in the sense of branches abiding in the vine, bring upon its life currents, loving Christ and keeping His commandments, and thereby enjoying His manifested presence, love and communion; "walking not after the flesh, but after the spirit," gaining the victory over the world through faith, etc., etc.

This new life begins with repentance, and the purposed forsaking of all sin; with accepting Jesus as the only ground of pardon, and moreover as the promised source of spiritual strength for holy living, and with a free consecration of all to God—a consecration absolute, unlimited, to be carried out and applied to the utmost extent of perceived duty.

The term sanctification may fitly be used in a sense somewhat broader than the term consecration; the latter being usually, perhaps naturally, limited to an act of the will; while sanctification may (perhaps commonly does) include the adjustment of the sensibilities—every appetite, passion, impulse, whether of body or mind, to this new law of the spiritual life. So understood sanctification involves progress in at least these three respects: ($a$) progressive knowledge of God and duty. ($b$) progressive adjustment of the sensibilities, $i.\ e.$ the impulses, propensities, and also the habitudes of mind and body, to the better understanding of the law of Christ, and to the demand of the spirit of full consecration. ($c$) A growing confirmation of these habitudes of the whole being, resulting in new accessions of strength, in greater safety against lapsing, and in general in a growing experience in this new life unto God.

And yet in some measure as an exception to this common law of progress, great crisis may occur in the Christian life.

A new and juster view of Christ's power to lift the soul into victory, through faith, may bring a great and sudden change into one's experience, memorable, perhaps enduring. There were obviously such sudden experiences in the great Pentecostal baptism of the Holy Ghost. And such experiences among the early Christians gives the possibilities of every convert from that day to this. If properly taught he may receive the Holy Ghost in precious baptisms at first, and may retain them from the first even until death. His first conversion and his second would thus become one and the same.

The nature of the case creates no necessity for a first conversion which shall lack the baptism of the Spirit, and a second at some subsequent day which shall bring it. He may have both of them at once. Nothing in the nature either of the human soul or the spirits functions, forbids this, and requires a first conversion without this baptism, and a second with it. But it seems to be a great and dangerous error to maintain that one act of faith can introduce the soul into such full sanctification, and guarantee its continuance, either permanently or for an indefinite time. For no one moral act can determine with absolute certainty all subsequent moral acts. It is also unscriptural and dangerous to substitute one act of faith for a whole life of faith ; one great act of prayer ; one effort of the will, however intense, however mighty, for a whole life of efforts.

(20) HIGHEST PRACTICAL PIETY ATTAINABLE IN THIS LIFE.

Now if the preceding explanations concerning sanctification and the subjects related to it be kept in mind, it will be readily perceived that in advocating the following proposition, we advocate only the attainability of such a type of piety as is both reasonable and practical. It will be understood that in maintaining the attainability of entire sanctification in this life, we advocate merely the attainment of such a high degree of piety as has been attained, and such as all Christians may attain, by faith in Christ in the present life. In other words, we regard the phrases entire sanctification in this life, and the highest practical piety, as synonymous phrases. And if any reader of this treatise should associate in his mind with the doctrine of entire sanctification in this life, either angelic perfection or human infallibility, it is not the writer's meaning. And it is only on the admission of the correctness of the preceding explanations concerning this scriptural doctrine, that we can expect to establish its truthfulness. And it cannot be expected that men can infallibly decide for each other in reference to their personal attainments, because they do not always agree in reference to what acts are sinful and what are innocent.

(21) PROPOSITION.

But assuming that all honest seekers for the highest attainments in practical piety shall accept the correctness of the preceding definitions and explanations, I maintain in the guarded language of one of its ablest advocates, the following proposition:

"Entire sanctification in this life is attainable in such a sense that all Christians should earnestly seek it, with the rational expectation of attaining it."

By this I mean that all Christians should obey God

in becoming as holy as possible in this life, and that such piety is all that the claims of God's law require. Now it is the common belief of intelligent and devoted Christians that we should aim to attain entire sanctification in this life, although it is unreasonable (in their opinion) to expect its attainment. But others believe that we should aim at it, with the rational expectation of attaining it in the present life. All believe that we must attain it, before we enter heaven. But as death does not change moral character, we should trust in the blood of the atonement here to cleanse us from all sin.

(22) PROOF OF ATTAINMENT.

If it ever has been attained, it may be attained again. "Noah was a just man, and perfect in his generation." "He walked with God." He attained a complete Christian character. He was entirely sanctified in this life. Said the inspired apostle to the Romans, "But now being made free from sin, and become servants to God, ye have your fruit unto holiness. For when ye were the servants of sin, ye were free from righteousness." Before conversion, they were in a state of entire sinfulness. Afterwards, they attained a state of entire freedom from it. The terms freedom from sin and freedom from righteousness, are not limited. Before conversion they had no holiness. At the time of conversion, as "the blood of Christ cleansed them from all unrighteousness," they were entirely freed from sin for the time being. And being made free from sin, they were delivered from its dominion, and from bondage to it, in the same sense and as absolutely, as before conversion they were free from righteousness. This service of entire consecration ensures holiness in this life, as really and entirely as consecration to worldliness and self-gratification did sin. Zechariah, and Elizabeth also, " were both righteous before God, walking in all the commandments and ordinances of the Lord blameless." These words refer to all the duties of religion which were made known to them. In the view of the "Searcher of Hearts," no deficiency could be found in them. They were strict and exact in all things. At heart they were in a state of entire holiness. Said the apostle to the Philippians, " Let us therefore, as many as be perfect, be thus minded."

(23) GOSPEL PROVISIONS.

Moreover, we are encouraged to make diligent efforts to obtain this same blessing through faith, in view of the gospel provisions. Sanctification is as much the object of Christ's atonement, as our justification. He came to save us, just as much from sin, as from its penalty. " Thou shalt call his name Jesus, for he shall save his people from their sins." " Who gave Himself for us, that He might redeem us from all iniquity, and purify unto Himself a peculiar people, zealous of good works."

(24) PRAYERS OF JESUS CHRIST.

Furthermore, we are encouraged to expect success in our efforts for this blessing, by the prayers of Christ in our behalf. " Sanctify them through Thy truth," prays Our Lord. "I pray that Thou shouldst keep them from the evil; that is, cleanse them from sin, make them pure in heart in Thy sight. Keep them from the power of temptation, from evil thoughts, passions and wicked desires—in a state of holiness."

(25) PRAYER OF PAUL.

Also the Apostle Paul prayed under inspiration, not for the sanctification of Christians at death, but in this life. "The very God of peace sanctify you wholly, and I pray God your whole spirit, and body and soul, be preserved blameless unto the coming of our Lord Jesus Christ. Faithful is he that calleth You, who also will do it." Here the apostle, it seems, "either offered an inspired prayer for the death of Christians, if they could not be sanctified until death, or else he offered the prayer of faith, by the assistance and direction of the Holy Ghost, that they might be completely sanctified in every part of their nature, and be preserved blameless in this life." He certainly had full assurance of its accomplishment, for he says, "Faithful is he that calleth You, who also will do it."

As Rev. Mr. Barnes explains this passage, "He prays, 'Sanctify you wholly,' in every part completely. He prays that God would make His people entirely holy. And in this he recognizes the truth that we have a body; we have animal life and instincts, in common with the inferior creation; and we have also a rational and immortal soul. The soul is the vital principle, while the animal life, or the seat of the senses, desires, affections, and appetites, we have in common with other animals. The mere animal life is distinct from the soul, as the seat of conscience and moral agency. Hence it is the duty of man to bring his whole nature under law, or so control it that it may not be an occasion of sin. And the apostle prayed that Christians might become entirely holy, and be kept from transgression, until the Lord Jesus came ; that is, either to remove them by death, or to wind up the affairs of this lower world."

God is faithful, who also will do it, as he has begun a work of grace in your hearts, you may depend on His faithfulness to complete it.

### (26) OBJECTIONS.

But in other portions of the Scriptures we read, " There is not a just man upon earth, that doeth good and sinneth not." " If we say we have no sin, we deceive ourselves and the truth is not in us." Certainly, a God of truth cannot contradict Himself, and he has said of some Christians " Ye are dead unto sin, alive unto righteousness." May not such seeming contradictions be reconciled by applying the former texts to all unregenerate men, and the latter to the regenerate ? He teaches us that both by nature are " dead in trespasses and sins," and that the most holy of Christians, as well as the worst of sinners, were by nature children of wrath," and that " he that committeth sin is of the devil." " But whosoever is born of God, doth not commit sin, for His seed remaineth in him, and he cannot sin because he is born of God." If the passages which state the universal sinfulness of men apply to all the regenerate, to whom do the passages apply which state that some are sinners? For in immediate connection with the passage which states "If we say we have no sin we deceive ourselves, and the truth is not in us," it reads, "If we confess our sin, He is faithful and just to forgive us, and to cleanse us from all unrighteousness." Of course, if any man shall say he has not sinned, and does not need the blood of atonement, he is mistaken. It seems to me that neither class of these very strong passages should be pressed too literally and strictly, without reference to their connection and scope, lest they involve the Scriptures in irreconcilable contradiction and absurdity. When it reads that the new-born soul cannot sin, it merely means that having passed from a state of habitual rebellion against the divine government, sin and rebellion are inconsistent with his new disposition and rule of life, contrary to his habitual designs, to follow the leadings of the Holy Spirit in striving with singleness of aim to please his Heavenly Father in all things. If, for instance, a merchant says he cannot take a reduced price for his merchandise, I understand him to mean that he cannot consistently, with his disposition to trade, so as to promote his business interests. I understand that it is in reality possible for him to do it, but it would be unreasonable. Hence I do not suppose that a justified or sanctified Christian can sacrifice his free agency, so as to be incapable of yielding to temptation. On a certain occasion, when the apostle was considering the doctrine of future resurrection, he says in reference to himself: "Not as though I had already attained, either were already perfect, I press toward the mark for the prize;" he may have meant also that he had not attained a state of freedom from sin. But he says to his brethren, in this immediate connection; "let us therefore, as many as be perfect, be thus minded." Intimating that some might have made the attainment of a more complete Christian character than those who were merely justified.

(27) PAUL'S EXPERIENCE.

After his own first radical conversion and complete justification, he seems to have been involved in a fearful conflict with temptation, and to have sometimes fallen under its fearful power; "for that which I do, I allow not, but what I hate, that I do." The strength of natural passion overcame him in unguarded circumstances. The power of the former habits of sin before conversion kept up a fearful and dreadful conflict with conscience, and the powers of darkness brought him under legal bondage. Afterward having said, "we know the law is spiritual," "for I delight in the law of God after the inward man," he seems to have had a new and refreshing experience of the power of divine grace in delivering him from his bondage under the adversary. He exclaims, "O wretched man that I am! who shall deliver me from the body of this death? 'I thank God through Jesus Christ our Lord.' There is therefore now no condemnation to them which are in Christ Jesus, who walk not after the flesh, but after the spirit." In this new and second experience, the Gospel has accomplished a complete deliverance, and gives the captive in sin a glorious and complete triumph over the enslaving power of temptation and furnishes abiding peace and holiness.

### (28) THE TRUSTFUL FORTIFIED.

Therefore if the scriptures teach that some Christians have gained not only repeated, but continuous victories over temptation, may not all Christians who are aiming to follow Him fully "who did no sin," entertain the rational hope of success in attaining this blessing in the present life, by faith and not by works? Has not God assured such as trust in Him with sufficient confidence, that he is ready to fortify them against the three great sources of temptation; the world, the flesh and the devil? "This is the victory that overcometh the world, even our faith." "Walk in the spirit and ye shall not fulfill the lusts of the flesh." "Above all taking the shield of faith, whereby ye shall be able to quench all the fiery darts of the wicked." "And the God of peace shall bruise Satan under your feet shortly." " Now our Lord is able to keep you from falling, and to present you faultless before the presence of His glory with exceeding joy." And can it be possible that Christians are unreasonable in fully trusting His ability and willingness to fulfill His offers and pledges to the utmost? "Having therefore these promises, dearly beloved, let us cleanse ourselves from all filthiness of the flesh and spirit, perfecting holiness in the fear of God." " Let us not be weary in well doing, for in due season we shall reap if we faint not." Let us not defer this invaluable attainment of grace through faith, for the weakness, the delirium, the expiring agonies of dissolving nature, when flesh and heart shall fail, and be incapable of purifying our moral and religious characters.

### (29) MEANS OF ATTAINMENT.

Therefore let us imitate strictly and constantly our Divine Redeemer, " who left us an example, that we should follow His steps." In so doing we must be entirely consecrated to the same benevolent ends which controlled Him in life and in death, and prosecute them with the same purity of intention, in our humble circumstances of weakness and temptation. " If therefore thine eye be single, thy whole body shall be full of light." We must have His spirit of meekness, resignation, humility, obedience, devotion and industry in doing good. We must habitually seek for grace to live and to act in all our changing circumstances and spheres, just as we think He would act, were He again in the flesh, in our places, surrounded by our temptations. In this way we shall be " changed into the same image from glory to glory even as by the spirit of the Lord." We must attain entire sanctification in this life by repeated and continued acts of faith. For sanctification as well as justification is by faith and not by works. It is by faith in the aids of divine grace and not by works of the law.

### (30) GOOD RESOLUTIONS AND FAITH.

Thus we shall engage in the daily duties of life, with the fixed purpose of fulfilling them perfectly to our utmost ability in the strength of our covenant-keeping

God, who has promised to make us victorious over temptation, and render us "more than conquerors through Him that loved us, and gave Himself for us, that He might redeem us from all iniquity." Thus we shall lead a new life, avoiding ostentation, practicing charity and striving in every way to lead an upright and honest life. Thus we shall find it even better to hope than to faint, knowing that good intentions must bear fruit in holy living, and that we have not resolved in vain, for good intentions must ever give character to all good works. We must expect to overcome each temptation by specific acts of faith in our Lord's assistance, for "this is the victory that overcometh the world, even our faith." We must not expect by one single act of faith to escape forever the warfare with temptation. But every new temptation will demand a specific act of faith to overcome such temptation. We must ever in this life "watch and pray that we enter not into temptation."

(31) TESTIMONY.

And are not all Christians who enjoy this precious religious experience, who are conscious that such is the daily intention and practice of their lives, with no self-righteous boasting with regard to their gracious attainments, knowing their fallibility in judging of their motives and experiences, justified in confessing it for the encouragement of all who may be earnestly seeking the blessing? Is it not highly proper, if not an imperative duty, under such circumstances, to testify in all humility to the praise of divine and all-conquering grace, what the Lord hath done for them? But it obviously should not be done frequently, and never, if it can be well avoided, in a promiscuous assembly of such as have no heart for its just appreciation, for it will be misunderstood and be perverted. "Give not that which is holy unto the dogs, neither cast ye your pearls before swine." But it must be right to imitate the devout and humble Psalmist of Israel, in prudently and for good reasons relating Christian experience, and growth in holy living. Said this inspired and holy man, "Come and hear, all ye that fear God, and I will declare what He hath done for my soul." The blind man, whom our Lord restored to sight, gave God the praise. "One thing I know, that whereas I was blind, now I see." Said the apostle, "I can do all things through Christ, which strengtheneth me." "The strength of sin is the law." "But thanks be to God, which giveth us the victory, through our Lord Jesus Christ." "If we love one another, God dwelleth in us, and His love is perfected in us." "Herein do I exercise myself to have always a conscience, void of offence toward God and toward man." "I have lived in all good conscience before God until this day." "For our rejoicing is this, the testimony of our conscience, that in simplicity and Godly sincerity, by the grace of God, we have had our conversation in the world."

(32) GOOD FRUITS.

The aim and expectation of attaining the highest practical holiness in this life, naturally as well as graciously, increases Christian purity and uprightness. This doctrine must be tested by its legitimate

*18

fruits, and be appreciated according to its obvious tendencies and results. Do not all intelligent and growing Christians consider it their imperative duty and exalted privilege to grow in grace and be sanctified through the truth? To live habitually in imitation of Christ, who " did no sin," and as the best of the primitive Christians did, according to the Scriptures? Yes; all, I trust, maintain that we should perseveringly endeavor to keep all the divine commandments as the unalterable rule of life. " For whoso keepeth His word, in him verily is the love of God perfected." But we go further than this, and maintain that we should not only aim to love God supremely and obey him strictly always, but we are authorized in the Scripture promises to really expect through God's all-sufficient grace, and by all-conquering faith in the help of Jesus, to habitually and uniformly obey him from the heart, with most positive strictness as the rule of life, according to the grace and strength given unto us. Jesus saith, " Believe ye that I am able to do this?" "According to your faith be it unto you." And the Apostle Paul said, "I can do all things through Christ, which strengtheneth me." And will not such aim, united with such expectation ensure better success in absolute attainment of heart purity, than an indefinite aim with no honest expectation of attaining definitely the highest practical standard of piety? Will not the practical and skillful marksman be more likely to really hit his game, or come much nearer to it, with a definite and absolute expectation, than he who merely points his gun at some indefinite region in the skies above, with no real expectation of reaching the mark? Let us therefore seek definitely the highest point of attainment, with the earnest spirit of the apostle who, with Moses, " had respect unto the recompense of reward." " This one thing I do, forgetting those things which are behind and reaching forth unto those things which are before, I press toward the mark for the prize." And " if the righteous scarcely be saved," so as by fire, who are merely justified, and there can be no purification in the process of death, let us earnestly and persistently strive to be entirely sanctified by faith, through the truth, and by the agency of the Holy Ghost in this life. " For so an entrance shall be ministered unto you abundantly into the everlasting kingdom of our Lord and Saviour, Jesus Christ." There can be no reasonable doubt that the Scriptures furnish reliable encouragement that all real Christians, who are truly penitent for their sins, shall be admitted to heaven. For it is written, " Be thou faithful unto death, and I will give thee a crown of life." " Being justified freely by His grace, through the redemption that is in Christ Jesus," all who persevere in a life of holiness shall be saved. For God " will render to every man according to his deeds. To them who by patient continuance in well-doing seek for glory and honor and immortality, eternal life." All who obey God, by submission to His authority, and are willing to obey the law by forsaking all their sins, are candidates for heaven. But the command is, " Strive to enter in at the strait gate; for many, I say unto you, will seek to enter in, and shall not be able."

# THE WORK OF THE HOLY SPIRIT. BY DR. WM. PATTON.

## (SANCTIFICATION.)

The Greek word is, in the New Testament, always rendered either sanctification or holiness. The idea of moral purity is expressed in all. The primitive word denotes separation from a common condition and use, to that which is special and sacred, implying dedication, and carries with it the idea of purity, of sanctity, of cleansing. There are three senses in which the word is used by the sacred writers. These are, (1) To acknowledge and celebrate as holy which is so in itself. Thus it is to be understood whenever God is said to be sanctified. (2) To separate or set apart time, things, or persons, from a common to a sacred use; thus the seventh day and the Sabbath, the Tabernacle and places of worship; also the sacramental elements are sanctified. (3) To make persons holy, who are impure and defiled. Thus the apostle uses the word (I. Cor. vi: 2), " And such were some of you; but ye are washed, but ye are sanctified, but ye are justified, in the name of the Lord Jesus, and by the spirit of our God." This is the meaning of the word, where the elect are said to be sanctified. It is this process by which a converted sinner is advanced from a lower to a higher state of purity, until he attains its highest elevation that is meant by the word sanctification, and which we now propose to illustrate. Guided by the word of God, the process of sanctification appears very simple. It is secured by obedience to the truth. I. Peter, i: 22—" Seeing ye have purified your souls in obeying the truth through the spirit, unto unfeigned love of the brethren." Here obedience on the part of man is indispensable. " Ye have purified your souls in obeying the truth." Peter felt no difficulty in telling those to whom he wrote that they had done it; that they, personally and individually, had actually purified their own souls—that they had done it freely and voluntarily, by obeying the truth. While he points out human activity and freedom, and the instrumentality of revealed truth, he honors the official agency of the Holy Ghost by declaring that their obedience to the truth was " through the spirit." He further gives the certain evidence of the reality of this purification, in that it secures " the unfeigned love of the brethren." The importance of human vigilance and activity is constantly enforced. I. John, i: 18—" But he that is begotten of God keepeth himself, and that wicked one toucheth him not." James, i: 27—" And keepeth himself unspotted from the world." The instrumentality of the truth is also made prominent. Our Lord said to His disciples (John, xv: 3), " Now are ye clean through the word which I have spoken unto you." In his prayer (John, xvii: 17), he thus pleads : " Sanctify them through Thy truth ; Thy word is truth;" verse nineteen: " And for their sakes I sanctify myself, that they also might be sanctified through the truth." The divine efficiency is most clearly stated. Both Paul and Peter use the same words when speaking of the election of sinners. II. Thess., i: 13, and I. Peter, i: 2—" Through sanctification of the spirit." Romans, xv: 16—" That the offering up of the Gentiles might be acceptable, being sanctified by the Holy Ghost." By reading the following passages together, we have a perspicuous view of all the agencies and instrumentalities required in the work of sanctification. II. Thess. ii: 13-14—"But we are bound always to give thanks to God for you, brethren, beloved of the Lord, because God hath from the beginning chosen you to salvation, through sanctification of the spirit and belief of the truth; whereunto he called you by our gospel to the obtaining of the glory of our Lord Jesus Christ." I. Peter, i: 2—"Elect, according to the foreknowledge of God the Father, through sanctification of the spirit, unto obedience and sprinkling of the blood of Jesus Christ;" verse twenty-second: "Seeing ye have purified your souls in obeying the truth through the spirit, unto unfeigned love of the brethren." Sanctification then, is obtained by obeying the truth, and this obedience is secured by the efficient agency of the Holy Spirit. The divine command may be clearly before the mind, but the duty which it requires, or the thing which it forbids, may be displeasing, as it crosses our plans or interferes with our pleasures. It may call for the sacrifice of some loved object, and we feel disinclined to obey. If left to ourselves, we will disobey, and continue to disobey, and thus wander further and further from God. But "through the spirit" we are led to obey—to obey willingly and cheerfully. By this obedience to the truth we yield to it, and the victory is gained. Thus we reverence the authority of God; right principles are strengthened, and our mind and will are brought more and more under the mind and will of God. When our mind and will are brought perfectly under the mind and will of God, so that our obedience is prompt, and cheerful, and universal, then our sanctification is complete. We know that in every regenerate person the light has begun to shine, and that " the path of the just is as the shining light which shineth more and more unto the perfect day."—Prov. iv: 18. Revealed truth is the instrumentality which the Holy Ghost uses in enlightening the mind, in operating upon the conscience, in purifying the affections, in subduing the will, and in securing the entire renovation and sanctification of the sinner. In conversion the Holy Ghost maintains His energizing of the faculties, and in addition exerts such an influence or agency to secure the change of the disposition the ruling purpose, so that the sinner now voluntarily loves what he before voluntarily hated. This agency, while it subdues the hatred and secures the love, is such that the freedom and activity of choice is not violated in the least possible degree, but is actually made more free and active. In sanctification, the Holy Ghost energizes the faculties, so that the truth is brought into living contact with the mind, producing the clear conviction of duty. Still, a further agency is needed, and exerted to secure obedience to the truth. By this free, cheerful, loving obedience, the soul is purified, or sanctified, or advanced in holiness.

(34) HOW TO OVERCOME SIN. BY PRES. FINNEY.

In every part of my ministerial life, I have found many professed Christians in a miserable state of bondage to the world, the flesh and the devil. But surely this is no Christian state, for the apostle distinctly said: " Sin shall not have dominion over you, because ye are not under the law, but under grace." In all my Christian life, I have been pained to find so many Christians living in the legal bondage described in the seventh chapter of Romans,—a life of sinning, and resolving to reform, and falling again.

### VICTORY BY FAITH.

But the Bible expressly teaches us that sin is overcome by faith in Christ. " He is made unto us wisdom, righteousness, sanctification and redemption." " He is the way and the truth and the life." Christians are said to " purify their hearts by faith."—Acts, xv: 9. And in Acts, xxvi: 18, it is affirmed that the saints are sanctified by faith in Christ. In Romans, ix: 31-32, it is affirmed that the Jews attained not to righteousness, " because they sought it not by faith, but as it were by the works of the law." The doctrine of the Bible is that Christ saves His people from sin through faith; that Christ's spirit is received by faith to dwell in the heart. It is faith that works by love. Love is wrought and sustained by faith. By faith Christians " overcome the world, the flesh and the devil." It is by faith that they " quench the fiery darts of the wicked." It is by faith that " they put on the Lord Jesus Christ, and put off the old man with his deeds." It is by faith that we fight " the good fight," and not by resolution. It is by faith that we "stand," by resolution we fall. This is the victory that overcometh the world, even our faith. It is by faith that the flesh is kept under and carnal desires subdued. The fact is that it is simply by faith that we receive the spirit of Christ to work in us, to will and to do, according to His good pleasure. He sheds abroad His own love in our hearts, and thereby enkindles ours. Every victory over sin is by faith in Christ; and whenever the mind is diverted from Christ, by resolving and fighting against sin, whether we are aware of it or not, we are acting in our own strength, rejecting the help of Christ, and are under a specious delusion. Nothing but the life and energy of the Spirit of Christ within us can save us from sin, and trust in the uniform and universal condition of the working of this saving energy within us. How long shall this fact be at least practically overlooked by the teachers of religion? How deeply rooted in the heart of man is self-righteousness and self-dependence? So deeply that one of the hardest lessons for the human heart to learn is to renounce self-dependence and trust wholly to Christ. When we open the door by implicit trust He enters in and takes up His abode with us and in us. By shedding abroad His love, He quickens our whole souls into sympathy with Himself, and in this way, and in this way alone, he purifies our hearts through faith. He sustains our will in the attitude of devotion. He quickens and regulates our affections, desires, appetites and passions, and becomes our sanctification.

### (35) HIGHEST AIM.

#### (EXTRACT.)

If you find yourselves disinclined to make strenuous efforts for the very highest definite attainments in holy living, " look into your Bible and see how Christians ought to live." See how the Bible says those who are Christians must live; and then if you find your professing Christian brethren living in a different way, instead of having cause for feeling that you may do so too, you have only cause to fear that they are deceiving themselves with the belief that they are Christians when they are not. Remember that the farther your Christian friends depart from the standard of Christian character laid down in the Bible, the less reason you have to hope that they are Christians. And do not hesitate upon this subject, because you find many professed Christians who are indifferent or lax in their practice and example. Remember that Christ has said, " many shall say unto me in that day, Lord, Lord," thus claiming to be His disciples, to whom He will say, " I never knew you."

### (36) APPLICATION.

#### (EXTRACT.)

There was never such an appeal to the divinest part of our nature, as in the times in which we are living, for personal purity; for disinterestedness; for holy self-denial; for joyfulness in suffering. There never was a time when men of fidelity to Christian truths would do so much to cheer the desponding, to inspire the drooping, to dissipate moral darkness, and to carry forward the work of God in the hearts of men, as in our time. Never was there such a test, such a dividing between the elect and the non-elect, as in the great providence which God is now instituting in this land. When I look out and see how men are bargaining and haggling; how they are forging chains of selfishness link by link; how they are studying still in the day of their country's anguish their own advancement and profit; and how their whole thought is "who shall show us any good?" my heart sinks in the contrast. Where are those that say, in the spirit of the Master, "for their sakes I sanctify myself?" Where are those that say, "It is not for me to become greater and richer; it is not for me to become personally more profited?" There is not necessarily any sin in this; but not to commit sin overtly, is not the motive which should actuate men now. In this time when Christ is sacrificed, and justice is brought into peril, and liberty itself is apparently in extreme danger, every Christian heart should say: "let my first thought and feeling of myself be to rise to a higher ambition, to higher endeavor, to higher courage, and to a truer esteem for God."

Everything for the cause of God, nothing for one's self. Everything for the divine kingdom, nothing for one's personal interest. Stand for the time, and the country, and the world, and the Church, and the eternity of God's cause. My brethren, we are called peculiarly to a personal application of these truths. It is a time for reviewing the past, and a time for forecasting the future. Never did Christians on the earth live in such an age, and under such motives, as now. All the past culminates in our day, and all the future, as it were, advances toward us, and calls to us. And what influence does all this have upon you? Are you called, in view of the past, in view of the exigencies of the present, and in view of the expectations of the future, to any difference of life? There is not a man, woman or child that has not a part in the great work that is being carried forward; and God calls you to perform that part. If you understand the call of God, in the time in which you live, you should sanctify yourselves for the sake of your day and generation. There never were more influential and potent reasons why every man should be a true Christian man, than now. I ask you, then, what repentance, what reformation is possible in your life? Are you willing to look in upon yourselves? Are you willing to search your hearts, clear down to the bottom? Are you willing to question your motives? Are you willing to go into the dark chamber of your experience? Are you willing to call God to go with you there? Are you willing to open the door of the sanctuary, and let blaze upon your secret thoughts and feelings, the whole light of the eternal throne, and say: "God, interpret to me my nature, my heart, my life, my character, my everything—that I may bring out whatever is evil in Thy sight, and for the sake of the world sanctify myself, and be a better man." It is quite in vain to talk about things in general. It is quite in vain to say, "I will, in general, look at sin." Will you look at it personally, man by man? Will you search your disposition trait by trait? Will you go through all your business, your pleasures, your affections—everything that relates to your happiness, or well-being, or to your misery and woe—and lay the law of God upon every part of your life with this solemn and earnest purpose: " I by the love of God,"—that shall not be withheld from any one of you—" am prepared to say in the presence of my Saviour, that I will sanctify myself for their sakes that are given me." Let it be so. And, as the housewife, taking her broom, begins and brushes every web however gauzy, out of the angle, and clears everything off from the windows and washes them, and sweeps in every corner and nook, and dusts in every alcove, and cleans every part, and gathers the collected dirt and marches it in a battalion towards the door and gradually works it through the hall and across the hall to the outside door, and, at last, with one blow, sweeps it all out and bids farewell to it; so let you hearts be cleansed. It is a good time to begin such a duty as this, and it is a good time to be faithful therein. And, for the sake of God, for the sake of the Church, for the sake of the family, and for the sake of the cause of God in our day, I call upon you to sanctify yourselves. What reformations in the performance of family duty toward your children do these thoughts suggest to you? Have you been such parents as you ought to have been? Have you set such an example before your children as you ought to have set? Have you taught them as you ought to have taught them? Have you borne with them and labored with them as you ought

*19

to have done? Are you doing it now—you that are in the midst of your life's calling? Are you carrying yourselves in the household so as to be a help to your children, or are you lying across the threshold so as to be a perpetual stumbling-block to them? Are you living with each other, husbands and wives, in the truest spirit of love, and in the largest sense of wedding? Are you one? or are you forever and forevermore two? Are you living to help each other, or to annoy each other? Are you living in the true excusatory spirit which always accompanies real conjugal love? Do you look upon each other, with all your faults and failings, as the heirs of God? In your hearts, made luminous by faith, do you see heaven blossoming in the face of your companions, and behold that which is to be, but which has not yet been, disclosed from the rubbish of imperfect human experience? And do you find yourselves moved to patience, to gentleness, and to holy forbearance? And are you every day twining around each other like two honeysuckles? And do the blossoms of your love send fragrance through all the dwelling and through every wedded day? Is there nothing to be done by you? Is there no change to be made in your life? If there are any here who are living in almost mortal hate, and who have formed habits of disagreement, then, if the root of your former love remains, do not destroy that but do as I did when I could not manage my old honeysuckle. I cut it off to the root, and in a few weeks it sent out new shoots; and I trained these new shoots as I wanted them to grow, and there they stand to my good pleasure.

And if your old love is gnarled and twisted, so that you cannot manage it, cut it off to the root, and cultivate new fruits of fresh love, that shall be for your happiness and profit. We talk about revivals in the Church. Oh, for a revival that shall make husbands and wives love each other, or that shall make those that do love each other more tolerant and patient toward one another! Oh, for a revival that shall lead husband and wife to take hold of hands, for their children's sake, and say: "Beloved, let us sanctify ourselves." Is there no work of this kind that is befitting you? Are there no thoughts in this connection that are applicatory to your business relations? Perhaps you say, some of you, " I conduct my business according to the best light I have." God be thanked if you do. I hope that there are some who can truly say this. But are there not some who need greater moderation? Honest you are, but are you not too intense, too much absorbed in your secular affairs? Do you not need to be more moderate in worldly things! Are you living up to the highest light that you have in this regard? Can you take the Word of God, and go through the processes of your business, and say, "There is nothing here that I am afraid to have God's eye rest upon?" Blessed are ye if it is so; but I exhort you, as your Christian friend, to take advantage of this great truth of which I have spoken, and say, ' In my business I am called of God, to sanctify myself for their sakes that are round about me, and to become a holier man in my secular administration." What new offices of labor, what new fidelities, what consecrations and purifications, are necessary that you may have more influence with those round about you, Sunday-school teacher? Are you as influential with your class as you would be if you were holier? You may avoid sins and faults of an overt kind, but are you not wanting in fervor, in heavenly mindedness, and in overflowing sweet dispositions? Are you not deficient toward those that are under your charge, because you lack so much of the grace of Christ Jesus? And is there not a call to you to sanctify yourselves this year, for their sakes that are committed unto your care? I invoke every one of you to a higher life for Christ's sake, for the sake of those around you, for the sake of the poor and needy in this land and in every land, for the sake of God who loves you, and for the sake of the Church Universal which is established for you. And this is my appeal; that you accompany me in the solemn confession of sin, and in the divinely implanted purpose of eradicating it root and branch; that you may look at yourselves as related to many parts of life; and that you take upon yourselves earnestly and irrevocably, for time and eternity, this solemn, this apostolic, this more than apostolic, this Christ-like example, and say, "For my own sake, for God's sake, and for the sake of all that live, I will sanctify myself." And God grant that having had a place in this earthly church, you and I may stand together in the church triumphant, without stain, or spot, or blemish, or any such thing, to the honor and the glory of the adorable name of Him by whom we are saved and in whom we trust. "Having therefore these promises," said the inspired apostle, "dearly beloved, let us cleanse ourselves from all filthiness of the flesh and spirit, perfecting holiness in the fear of God."

# CHAPTER XXXI.

## THE CHRISTIAN'S SECRET OF A HAPPY LIFE.

### (ABSTRACT.)

(1) The Lord has taught me experimentally and practically, certain lessons out of His word, which have greatly helped me in my Christian life, and have made it a very happy one. And I want to tell this lesson to others that they may have a happy life also. I cannot bear to keep the secret to myself.

### (2) GOD'S SIDE AND MAN'S SIDE.

God's part in the work of sanctification and man's part. Man's part is to trust, and God's part is to work. We are to be delivered from the power of temptation and sin, and are to be made "perfect in every good work to do the will of God." We are to "be transformed by the renewing of our minds, that we may prove what is that good and acceptable, and perfect will of God." The Lord Jesus Christ has come to do this work, and he will do it for all who put themselves wholly into His hand and trust Him to do it. In this highest Christian life, man trusts with his whole heart, and God does the thing entrusted to Him. Now, sanctification is both a sudden step of faith on our part, and also a gradual process on God's part. By a step of faith we put ourselves into the hands of Christ, and by a gradual process He prepares us for every good work. The maturity of Christian experience cannot be reached in a moment, but is the result of the work of the Holy Spirit. Sanctification as a present experience does not consist in maturity of growth, but in purity of heart, and this may be as complete in the babe in Christ as in the veteran believer. By a step of faith we put ourselves into the hands of the Lord, for Him to work in us all the good pleasure of His will, and by a continuous exercise of faith we keep ourselves there, yielding ourselves unto God and " He works in us, to will and to do of His good pleasure." " I labored, yet not I but the grace of God which was with me."

(3) THE LIFE DEFINED.

This highest, happiest life, is a life of trust; " hid with Christ in God." The Bible teaches us that our Saviour is as able to save from anxious care and the power of temptation as from the penalty of transgression. This exalted religious experience consists in simply trusting the Lord to carry our burdens and manage our affairs for us, instead of indulging anxious care in striving to manage our affairs ourselves, without trustfully looking to Him for aid. If we would be at peace we must take all our cares to Him and leave them there. We must trust in divine strength to support us under our burdens, every thing that troubles us, whether spiritual or temporal, whether inward or outward. After we have taken our trouble to the Lord and left it there, if it comes back, we must take it to Him again and leave it until we find perfect rest. " Be careful for nothing, and the peace of God which passeth all understanding shall keep your hearts and minds, through Christ Jesus." We must be teachable and trustful as little children. A young child trusts its devoted parent from years end to years end with no anxious solicitude. He provides nothing for himself, his parent provides everything; he lives peacefully from moment to moment. Hence our heavenly Father says to us, " Take no thought for yourselves. Trust in the Lord, and do good, so shalt thou dwell in the land, and verily thou shalt be fed."

(4) HUNGERING AND THIRSTING FOR RIGHTEOUSNESS.

Our Divine Redeemer has said: " Blessed are they which do hunger and thirst after righteousness, for they shall be filled."

(ABSTRACT.)

This is God's policy of insurance upon the enterprise of right living. It presents Him as saying: " Take any other ideal of life, and you take risks as to succeeding. But if you will make it always your supreme choice to live aright, I pledge myself that you shall have success." For the effort to live aright is the one effort, among all the varieties of human strivings, which cannot be frustrated by hindrances outside of one's self. In the various aspirations and undertakings of mankind, there is no certainty of succeeding; the utmost wisdom and earnestness of endeavor do not always accomplish the result. Health? One may understand the conditions and laws which promote good health, and observe them to the utmost, yet accidents unforeseen may derange the organization, unpreventable exposure may cause disease, one's wisely chosen food or medicine may poison him with unknown adulterations, and old age will surely bring infirmities and decay. Wealth? A merchant may understand the laws of commerce, may plan his business judiciously, live frugally, save steadily, and invest wisely; the failure and frauds of others may overwhelm him. Fame? One may desire to the utmost the good opinion of others, and live circumspectly to that end, yet the jealousies of rivals or enemies may involve him in undeserved obloquy. Usefulness? One may engage sincerely, earnestly, and steadily in some well-planned scheme of doing good, yet circumstances wholly unforeseen and uncontrollable, may defeat the plan. Power? How many men, endowed with apparent qualification and favorable circumstances to attain power, have utterly failed while doing the best that could be done? But a wise, unyielding effort for righteousness, in the eye and appreciation of God, is righteousness. Hence, when one knows what is right, and strives perseveringly to do it, trusting in divine assistance, that effort cannot be defeated. In really hungering and thirsting for righteousness, "he shall be filled." But it must be something more than the pleasureable anticipations which brings us to our daily meals. It must be real craving, hunger and thirst for rectitude, an inflexible and earnest desire and purpose, so overwhelming above and beyond all other hopes and objects, as to ensure its gratification in right living in preference to all sinful indulgences.

(5) HOW TO ENTER IN.

In order for a soul to be made into a vessel for God's honor, "sanctified and meet for the Master's use, and prepared unto every good work," it must be entirely consecrated and abandoned to Him, so as to become passive in His hands. The whole spirit, soul and body, must be surrendered to God's absolute and unconditional control. His directions must be implicitly followed. In every moral act the supreme choice must be "Thy will be done." In this spirit of entire submission we shall experience the happiest and most restful of lives. For God loves us, and knows what is best for us, and His way must be the best for us under all circumstances. Faith is the next thing. Faith is an absolutely necessary element in the reception of any gift; for, let our friends give a thing to us ever so fully, it is not really ours until we believe it has been given, and claim it our own. Love may be lavished upon us by another, but until we believe that we are loved, it never really becomes ours. In the beginning of the Christian life, we believed that Jesus was our Saviour from the penalty of sin, and according to our faith it was unto us. Now we must believe that He is our Saviour from the power of temptation, and according to our faith it shall be unto us. Then we were justified by faith, now we must take Him as a Saviour from the bondage of sin. But sometimes the earnest Christian, desiring entire sanctification, cannot believe that he is entirely consecrated until he feels that he is. He puts feeling first, and faith second. Now God's invariable rule is, faith first and feeling afterward, in everything. He should give himself to God entirely, definitely, fully, according to his present light, asking the Holy Spirit to show him all that is contrary to God, either in heart or life. If He shows anything, give it to the Lord immediately, and say in reference to it, "Thy will be done." Do you, then, at this moment, surrender yourself wholly to Him? Then He has taken you, and He "is working in you to will and to do His good pleasure." It is your purpose God appreciates, not your feelings about that purpose. Pure religion resides in the will alone. As the will is the governing power in man's nature, if the will is set strait all the rest of man's nature must come into harmony. If then God is reigning there by the power of His Spirit, all the rest of our nature must be obedient to Him. "If any man shall do His will he shall know of the doctrine." Your entire sanctification is attained, not because your faith in itself sanctifies you, but because it links you to your Saviour, who is "called Jesus, because He shall save His people from their sins." He is able to save to the uttermost. " The blood of Jesus Christ cleanseth from all sin." Now God says, "Yield yourselves unto Me, as those that are alive from the dead, and I will work in you to will and to do of My good pleasure." And the moment that we yield ourselves, He of course takes full possession of us, and does work in us that which is pleasing in His sight, through Jesus Christ, giving us the mind that was in Christ, and transforming us into His image. In this way we shall become wholly the Lord's, and have the witness of the spirit that He sanctifies us through the truth. We shall trust in the blood of Jesus as a sufficient atonement for all past sins, and we shall commit the future wholly to the Lord, agreeing to do His will under all circumstances, as He shall make it known. We shall trust Him for a present supply of grace, and trust Him in the future to keep us from sin from moment to moment. Nothing else will take all the risks and supposes out of the Christian life, and enable him to say: "Surely goodness and mercy shall follow me all the days of my life." And such a soul can say:

> "I know not what it is to doubt,
> My heart is always gay,
> I run no risk, for come what may,
> God always has His way."

If the will of God is our will, and He always has His way, then we always have our way also, and we reign in a perpetual kingdom. If we side with God we must triumph in every encounter, and whether the result shall be joy or sorrow, under all circumstances we shall join in the apostles shout of victory, " Thanks be unto God, which always causeth us to triumph in Christ."

(6) GROWTH IN GRACE.

When the earnest seeker has really entered into this exalted Christian life, " which is hid with Christ in God," by entire surrender and confiding trust he must aim constantly at spiritual progress, and at future increase and development as he advances in the divine life. He must advance from the feebleness of infancy toward the strength of mature manhood, so as to bring forth ripe fruit. Do not trouble yourselves about growing, but trust in Christ continually for your growing life, that He may work in you all the good pleasure of His will. Put your growing life in His hands for its progress and completion, " and the peace of God, which passeth all understanding, shall keep your hearts and minds, through Christ Jesus." " Abide in me and I in you. As the branch cannot bear fruit of itself, except it abide in the vine, no more can ye, except ye abide in me." " The righteous shall flourish like the palm tree ; he shall grow like the cedar in Lebanon." Therefore you must increase in holiness, advance in piety. Though your spiritual life be now as feeble as the physical and intellectual life of an infant, it must strengthen with your strength and grow with your growth. You must increase in the fervor and constancy of your love to God and submission to His holy and righteous will.

*20

### (7) SERVICE.

When a Christian enters into the hidden life with Christ in God, he experiences a great change in the matter of service. In all the lower forms of Christian experience, service is apt to have much of bondage in it. The conscience of the Christian urges him to obey the Divine law, merely from a sense of duty, and often his religious services are great trials and crosses. He finds his struggling experience in the seventh chapter of Romans: "For we know (says he) that the law is spiritual; but I am carnal, sold under sin. . . For to will is present with me; but how to perform that which is good, I find not." Now in these higher forms of Christian experience, the soul is in a great measure delivered from this species of bondage in proportion as he enters fully into the blessed life of faith. His improved experience is like that of the Apostle Paul in the eighth chapter of Romans. "For the law of the spirit of life hath made me free from the law of sin and death." They that are after the spirit, do mind the things of the spirit. To be spiritually minded is life and peace. When we come into this state, we do God's will with as much pleasure and heartiness as men in their unsanctified state do their own wills. As God works in us "to will and do of His good pleasure," we will what He wills, not merely because it is our duty, but because we delight to do His will as He desires. Says the Psalmist: "I delight to do Thy will." Says the Apostle: "I delight in the law of God." If this be our experience, let us habitually inquire, how shall I serve my Master to-day? Let us dedicate ourselves anew to Him body and soul and spirit, with all our possessions and influence. We must look to Him for all we need through the day. "If ye shall ask anything in My name, I will do it." We must imitate Jesus in all we do. We must do as we think He would do in our circumstances. We must speak of Him to all who will listen to our conversation, and walk with Him in peace and holiness. "Them that honor me, I will honor." Then let us follow our Lord's example by a life of self-sacrificing beneficence in " going about doing good."

(8) TEMPTATION.

Christian life is a continuous warfare with temptation. Great temptations are frequently a sign of great grace in the heart, consequently temptation is not sin. But in every temptation we must expect to conquer, for God says: "Be strong and of a good courage." Blessed is the man that endureth temptation, not in his own weakness and susceptibility, but by faith in the proffered strength of Almighty God. Resist the temptations of the world, the flesh and the devil. Walk through the fiercest assaults with unclouded and triumphant peace, knowing that " when the enemy shall come in like a flood, the spirit of the Lord shall lift up a standard against him." We must ever remember that sanctification is not a thing to be kept without the use of appropriate means in a certain stage of Christian experience, but it is a life to be lived day by day, and hour by hour. If at any time, by neglect of watchfulness, the strength of temptation and the weakness of faith, there be momentary stumbling in our walk, we must instantly regain our step by turning to Jesus, our continuous guide and unfailing support. There is no remedy to be found in discouragement. As well might a child who is learning to walk, lie down in despair when he has fallen, and refuse to take another step, as a believer, who is learning how to live and walk by faith, give up in despair because of having fallen into sin. The only way, in both cases, is to get up and try again, trusting to the sympathy and support of our loving father. By a penitential return to God for forgiveness for the past, and strength for the future, we may be sure of immediate forgiveness. "If we confess our sins, he is faithful and just to forgive us our sins, and to cleanse us from all unrighteousness. The Lord Jesus is able to deliver us out of the hands of our enemies, that we may serve him without fear in holiness and righteousness before him all the days of our life. Let us confidingly trust in God's offers of gracious support, that he will be able to make us perfect in every good work to do his will, working in us that which is well pleasing in his sight, through Jesus Christ, to whom be the glory forever and ever, Amen.

(9) PRACTICAL RESULTS.

If all that has been written concerning the life hid with Christ in God be true, its results in the practical daily walk and conversation ought to be very marked, and the Christians who have entered into the enjoyment of it, ought to be, in very truth, a peculiar people, zealous of good works. Such Christians must walk through the world as Christ walked. They must have the mind that was in him. They must possess meekness and quietness of spirit as characteristics of the daily life. With a submissive acceptance of the will of God in his dark and mysterious providences, they must do and suffer all the good pleasure of His will; there must be calmness and trust in the midst of turmoil, so as to be relieved from excessive anxiety and solicitude. Christians who thus walk with God will find joy and peace in believing. They will enjoy a foretaste of that rest which remaineth for the people of God in heaven. As it is written " eye hath not seen, nor ear heard, neither have entered into the heart of man the things which God hath prepared for them that love Him. But God hath revealed them unto us by His spirit."

# CONCLUSION.

## DIVINE MESSAGE.

### SERMON.

Text: "I have a message from God unto thee." "Prepare to meet thy God. Be ready. The time is short."

### INTRODUCTION.

"These are the words I spake unto you while I was with you, that after my decease ye might have them always in remembrance."

#### (1) PRECIOUS TRUTH.

The Bible, which commands all virtue, and forbids all sin, was given by inspiration of God, to make men wiser, better, and happier. Bad men would not make such a book of holy precepts, examples, and instructions, to condemn themselves, and good men, uninspired, could not teach " Thus saith the Lord," knowing it to be their own invention. Therefore, it was written by "holy men of God, as they were moved by the Holy Ghost;" for the conversion and sanctification of perishing sinners.

### (2) IMMORTALITY.

Jesus brought life and immortality to light. He said: " Because I live, ye shall live. He that believeth in me, though he were dead, yet shall he live." He shall never die.

### (3) RESURRECTION.

" All that are in their graves shall come forth ; they that have done good unto life, and they that have done evil unto condemnation." God will give us spiritual bodies, suited to their offices, " for He doeth whatsoever pleaseth Him."

### (4) JUDGMENT.

" After death the judgment " of every work, with every thing, good or evil. " The unjust will be unjust still, and the holy will be holy still."

### (5) HOLINESS SAFE. SIN DANGEROUS.

Sin and suffering exist here, under God's merciful government, and the compassionate Jesus says, hereafter the wicked " shall go away into eternal punishment."

### (6) SINS OF OMISSION.

"Inasmuch as ye did it not." "All have sinned and come short of the glory of God, being dead in trespasses and sins."

### (7) LOVE IN JUSTIFICATION.

"God so loved the world that He gave His only begotten Son, that whosoever believeth in Him should not perish." "By the law none shall be justified, but by grace through faith." "With the heart man believeth unto righteousness."

### (8) VICTORY BY FAITH.

"Watch and pray that ye enter not into temptation. God giveth us the victory through our Lord Jesus Christ. This is the victory that overcometh the world, even our faith."

### (9) WITNESS OF THE SPIRIT.

"We know that we love God, when we keep his commandments, and they are not grievous," when we delight to do His will, not from a mere sense of duty. If we find our experience in the fifty-first Psalm, and in the eighth of Romans, instead of the seventh, "we know that God abideth in us by the spirit He hath given us."

### (10) HEAVEN.

"The wise shall shine as the brightness of the firmament, and they that turn many to righteousness, as the stars forever and ever.

## CONCLUSION.

**HUMAN QUESTIONS WITH DIVINE ANSWERS.**

(APPEAL TO THE IMPENITENT.)

1. Why are you not a Christian?
"Ye will not come unto me, that ye might have life."

2. Do you fear what others may say of you?
"Whosoever shall be ashamed of me, of him shall the Son of Man be ashamed."

3. Do the faults of professing Christians hinder you?
"Every one of us shall give account of himself to God."

4. Are you willing to be lost, because the worst of professors are?
What are their faults to you? "Follow me," says our Lord.

5. Are you unwilling to consecrate all to Christ?
"What shall it profit a man if he gain the whole world, and lose his own soul? He that forsaketh not all that he hath, cannot be my disciple."

6. Do you fear that you will not be accepted?
"Whosoever will, let him take of the water of life freely."

7. Do you fear that you are too great a sinner?
"If we confess, and forsake our sins, He will cleanse us from all unrighteousness."

8. Are you afraid you may not persevere?
"He that hath begun a good work in you, will perform it."

9. Do you trust to good works?

"The Lord looketh on the heart," to see if it is your supreme aim to please Him in all things.

"Whosoever shall offend in one point is guilty" and condemned for breaking the law, for which morality cannot atone.

10. Do you ask what shall I do?

"Repent and make you a new heart. Believe on the Lord Jesus Christ, and thou shalt be saved. He that believeth not, the wrath of God abideth on him. Pray daily, 'God be merciful to me a sinner,' for Christ's sake.'"

11. Why delay?

"Boast not thyself of to-morrow. There is but a step between thee and death."

12. When should you begin to serve God?

"Choose you this day." "Now is the time."

13. What more can be done for you?

"What could have been done more than has been done? Jesus said, 'It is finished.'"

# SUPPLEMENT.

## A SKETCH

—OF THE—

## LIFE OF REV. WALTER P. DOE.

# PREFACE.

This brief sketch of the life of a Christian minister is prepared as a memorial for gratuitous circulation among his relatives and others, because it is thought that it contains some hints as the result of his experience, study and observation, which may benefit the living and instruct and stimulate them to diligence in the Christian life.

At the same time it is designed to perpetuate and disseminate some of the religious and reformatory truths which he regarded as very precious, and earnestly endeavored to promote by example and oral address, during life, so that after his decease the living may realize that " He being dead, yet speaketh."

As he experienced very many hindrances in life, which prevented him from accomplishing all the good which he strongly desired to do, it is hoped that the teachings and motives which influenced him may stimulate others to earnestness in doing good, and thus perpetuate his Christian and ministerial usefulness.

W. P. D.

Providence, R. I., January 1st, 1883.

# CONTENTS.

| | Page. |
|---|---|
| CHAPTER I. | |
| Early Life | 1 |
| CHAPTER II. | |
| Religious Experience | 2 |
| CHAPTER III. | |
| Residence in New York | 4 |
| CHAPTER IV. | |
| Devotion to Revivals and Moral Reform | 5 |
| CHAPTER V. | |
| Personal Efforts as a Layman | 6 |
| CHAPTER VI. | |
| Call to Preach. | 8 |
| CHAPTER VII. | |
| Student Life | 10 |
| CHAPTER VIII. | |
| Ministry | 12 |
| CHAPTER IX. | |
| Temperance | 14 |

## CONTENTS.

### CHAPTER X.
Slavery and the Civil War.................................. 16

### CHAPTER XI.
Domestic and Pecuniary Condition......................... 18

### CHAPTER XII.
Physical Disability............................................ 20

### CHAPTER XIII.
Fields of His Ministry........................................ 21

### CHAPTER XIV.
Faithfulness in View of Hindrances........................ 24

### CHAPTER XV.
Reflections and Anticipations............................... 30

### CONCLUSION.
Rewards Proportioned to Faithfulness..................... 32

# CHAPTER I.

## EARLY LIFE.

Rev. Walter P. Doe was born at Wilton, near Saratoga Springs, N. Y., on the 30th of March, A. D., 1813, of intelligent and energetic parents in prosperous circumstances. He was early taught the principles of economy, industry, and strict morality.

During the intervals of his attendance at school, he was much engaged in assisting and managing his father's extensive business.

After finishing his preparatory education at Johnstown Academy, at the age of eighteen, he engaged in learning the mercantile business, in Troy, N. Y.

## CHAPTER II.

### RELIGIOUS EXPERIENCE.

Although he had been seriously disposed from early youth, and had always designed that the world should be the better for his having lived in it, and had believed that true piety was of inestimable value and importance, in reforming the life and in affording consolation in affliction as well as in furnishing a sustaining hope in prospect of death, he was hindered for several years from engaging personally in the positive and active service of God by reason of the mystery which seemed to be thrown about regeneration by those who professed to have experienced it.

But, on leaving home to seek his fortune in the world, he was the subject of the increasing and special strivings of the Holy Spirit. He early yielded to His influence, and decided to renounce entirely all reliance upon his strict morality for salvation and

## RELIGIOUS EXPERIENCE.

trust unreservedly in the atonement of Jesus Christ, and lead a benevolent, prayerful, penitent, obedient and holy life.

In this reasonable and wise decision to enlist for time and eternity in the service of God, and in striving to please Him in all things, as the supreme and controlling purpose of life, he found abiding and increasing peace and satisfaction.

In his subsequent experience, he endeavored to obey the Divine injunction, " Grow in grace and in the knowledge of our Lord and Saviour Jesus Christ." Hence, in his Christian warfare with temptation, he was graciously sustained by faith in the Divine Redeemer. He aimed supremely, earnestly and perpetually at entire consecration and entire holiness, so as to walk in "the path of the just, which is as the shining light that shineth more and more unto the perfect day." And with this evidence of renewed and sanctified life he made a public profession of his faith in Christ on the first of January, 1832, in the Second Presbyterian Church in the city of Troy, where he then resided.

# CHAPTER III.

## RESIDENCE IN NEW YORK.

In the year 1833 he removed to the city of New York to engage in the employment of those distinguished Christian philanthropists and reformers, Messrs. Arthur Tappan and Company, who conducted one of the very largest and most honorable mercantile establishments of that period. Here he spent a few years in very active and absorbing business pursuits, and the employment of all his leisure hours in mental culture, by choice reading, or in the study of human nature, which the increased facilities of that populous city afforded.

# CHAPTER IV.

## DEVOTION TO REVIVALS AND MORAL REFORMS.

In this new relation to society in New York, he early became actively identified not only with genuine and powerful revivals of true religion, but having embraced the gospel as a reformatory and progressive system, he entered earnestly into the benevolent enterprises and great Christian reforms, which are designed to improve the condition of the oppressed, degraded and vicious classes of our own population, as well as of papal and heathen countries. From this period, not only the bible and tract causes, but the causes of domestic and foreign missions, and other similar societies, ever enlisted his warmest sympathies, prayers, efforts and contributions.

## CHAPTER V.

### PERSONAL EFFORTS AS A LAYMAN.

About this period, through the influence of Harlan Page and other devoted laymen, the duties and encouragements to personal efforts for the salvation of souls began to be more than usually recognized in the churches, and were greatly blessed in the conversion of sinners. As might have been expected in his youthful earnestness, he entered heartily into this commendable work, in proportion as his active business engagements permitted. His humble efforts, in the Sabbath School and in his tract district, as well as in the protracted religious meetings in periods of of revival influences, were much blessed in the awakening and conversion of several persons who have occupied influential positions as ministers and other office bearers, as well as active private members of the Church of Jesus Christ. In order to be successful in this work of faith and labor of love, he maintained that Christians should be in a very prayerful and spiritual frame of mind, so as to realize the very great importance of the conversion of individual sinners, and also to be able to discriminate between careless, awakened and deeply convicted sinners, so as to give to each appropriate instruction and exhortation, and thus secure their immediate conversion.

He maintained that Christians should seek favorable periods for exhorting the impenitent, when they are at leisure, when they are alone, or when they are in affliction. Also that the manner should be kind, earnest, plain and faithful, as well as personal. Their honest difficulties should be removed as far as possible, but there should be no debate in reference to caviling objections. If the sinner refers to the difference of sentiments among Christian denominations, he should be shown that all agree that faith in Christ is the only way to be saved. If he refers to the faults of Christians, he should be urged to strive to enter the strait gate for himself. He should be warned faithfully of the great sin of practical unbelief and of his sins of omission, as well as of his great danger, and the duty of immediate trust in Christ for salvation. He should be urged to renounce immediately and entirely all his worldly idols and choose the service of the Lord, heartily forsaking all known and willful sins, and with penitence and prayer obey all the divine requirements. With such efforts to save sinners, he believed that Christians of moderate gifts might succeed in persuading very many to choose the way of eternal life.

# CHAPTER VI.

## CALL TO PREACH.

And it was while sharing in precious and powerful revivals of religion, as the result of pungent preaching and prayerful personal efforts, that he thought that he received a divine call to prepare for the gospel ministry. But as providential circumstances seemed strongly to oppose his commencing the preparatory studies, while they offered very flattering and bright prospects for becoming permanently and successfully established in the mercantile business, he delayed for a few years the great change in his pursuits. But he often felt himself graciously called of God, as was Aaron, "to preach the gospel."

His feelings and experiences were like those of the prophet Jeremiah, when he said, "His word was in my heart, as a burning fire shut up in my bones, and I was weary with forbearing." He felt also like the apostle Paul, when he said, "Necessity is laid

## CALL TO PREACH. 9

upon me; yea, woe is me, if I preach not the gospel." He felt that the address of the sacred poet to the awakened sinner was applicable to himself in respect to his divine call to preach.

> "Those new desires, that in thee burn,
> Were kindled by His grace."

From that period, through the remainder of his active ministry, until the decline of life led him to retire from it, he always had an inexpressible earnestness and unquenchable passion for preaching the "glorious gospel of the blessed God." He felt habitually that he had rather preach the gospel than to attain the greatest riches of earth, or the most exalted human honors and felicities, or govern an empire, or sway the political destinies of a world. With such experiences, he consequently determined to abandon his flattering pecuniary prospects of permanently settling in New York, and go to the far West, and encounter much self-denial and privation for many years, in preparatory study, for the purpose of pursuing through life the humble and trying duties of the Christian ministry, with the deliberate expectation of very meagre pecuniary support, and that the experiences of his profession would be the source of the keenest sorrows as well as the greatest joys of any vocation in life. And these anticipations were fully confirmed in his subsequent experience. But he always felt in sympathy with the apostle Paul, in the exclamation: "I thank Christ Jesus our Lord, who hath enabled me, for that he counted me faithful, putting me into the ministry."

## CHAPTER VII.

### STUDENT LIFE.

In the year 1837 he began his preparatory studies at Quincy, Illinois, upon the banks of the Mississippi, under the instructions of that eminently devoted minister of Christ, Dr. David Nelson, the author of the "Cause and Cure of Infidelity," one of the most useful and interesting books ever written. During the vacations of study he was much blessed in revivals of religion, in places where no churches or ministers existed in that new country, then greatly destitute of the means of grace. Afterward he entered Oberlin College, Ohio, and was greatly benefitted by the instructions and influence of President Finney, whom he always regarded as one of the most holy, as well as one of the very greatest and most effective teachers and preachers. But in 1843, in

## STUDENT LIFE.

consequence of the death of his father, he returned to his eastern home, in Saratoga County, N. Y., to assist in the settlement of his estate. He afterwards entered Union College at Schenectady, N. Y., then under the presidency of Dr. Nott, one of the most eloquent of preachers, and a teacher of human nature of great sagacity, where he graduated in 1844. After spending three years at Union and Andover Theological Seminaries, he graduated at the latter institution, having enjoyed the valuable instructions of Prof. Park, so universally then, and for many years subsequently, recognized as the most erudite of theological teachers, and the most scholarly and eloquent of preachers.

# CHAPTER VIII.

## MINISTRY.

He was ordained in 1847 as an Orthodox Congregational Minister at River Point, R. I. From this period, after declining different calls for permanent settlement, that he might preach in different places in revivals, he alternately occupied the position of acting pastor of different churches, or visited the destitute, and preached much of the time at his own expense as an Evangelist. During his Academical, Collegiate and Theological studies, he obtained very clear views of the importance and practicability of eminent scriptural holiness in both the ministry and private membership of the church, in order to qualify them for the greatest efficiency in the vineyard of the Lord. Having also obtained what he regarded as sound and comprehensive views concerning God's paternal moral government over his intelligent creatures, and his readiness to grant the special effusions of His spirit, to give efficacy to appropriate, seasonable and pungent preaching, and the free agency of sinners and their obligation to repent and believe on Christ " with the heart unto righteousness," and choose the service of God immediately, his ministry was almost uniformly effective.

Being an eclectic in the pursuit of the most efficient means of promoting religion, and having had superior advantages for studying carefully the elements of power and secrets of success of many of the most effective revival preachers of the present century, he came early to the conclusion that a powerful ministry in spiritual results must be a pre-eminently holy ministry, and be constrained by the love of Christ and deep compassion for perishing sinners, so as with good judgment and discriminating sagacity to aim at and strive for, and confidently expect definite results in the revival of the work of grace in the hearts of the saints, and in the renewal and sanctification of sinners.

# CHAPTER IX.

## TEMPERANCE.

He adopted in early life the strict principles of temperance in all things,—the moderate use of things innocent and healthful, and total abstinence from all things intoxicating, poisonous and injurious. Hence he abstained not only from the use of all intoxicating drinks as a beverage, but from the use of all such narcotics as tobacco in any of its forms, and from the ordinary, unhealthful drinks of tea and coffee. And by such strict obedience to physical law, not only in diet and drinks, but in sleeping, cleanliness, toil and recreative exercise, as well as by endeavoring to look on the hopeful side of the future, he preserved in a great degree his general health and cheerfulness.

And when any phase of the temperance reformation gave encouragement for special efforts in behalf of moral suasion, or legal prohibition of the sale of liquors, he was accustomed to preach and publish in its favor, and he believed that the legislature should authorize each town, by a majority at a special meeting, to decide the question of legal prohibition, disconnected from all other issues, or make the sellers of liquor legally liable for all the damage of the sale. And he often spoke in public and private against the common use of tobacco as an injurious, expensive and filthy habit, paving the way to the use of intoxicating drinks and other vicious habits.

# CHAPTER X.

## SLAVERY AND THE CIVIL WAR.

In all the fierce conflicts in behalf of the rights of the enslaved, from his youth and from the very beginning of the modern agitation for more than thirty years, he bore a very active and laborious part in his sphere of life. As he firmly believed that our Lord's golden rule showed the system of American Slavery and all its legal enactments and natural consequences to be sinful, and that all the real friends of oppressed humanity should plead for the deliverance of the enslaved as they would rightfully desire them to labor for their freedom if the white race were in bondage, he maintained their cause in the early days of the discussion, when it demanded much personal sacrifice. He also advocated the cause of loyalty and liberty, from the pulpit and the press, during the gloomy disasters to our arms, when the conflict had culminated in civil war, and he urged a petition to

President Lincoln to issue the Emancipation Proclamation about the time he did issue it, which not only abolished slavery in our land, but secured the blessing of the Almighty in bringing the war to a victorious termination in favor of impartial freedom and the political citizenship of the colored race.

# CHAPTER XI.

### DOMESTIC AND PECUNIARY CONDITION.

In his domestic relations he was highly favored. Having married Miss Sophia S. Knight, of Providence, R. I., in 1849, who "looked well to the ways of her household," he was to a great extent relieved from ordinary family anxieties and was enabled to give himself wholly to study and the ministry of the word.

His pecuniary condition was commonly such that he was not distracted from the duties of his favorite profession by the embarrassments of poverty or the care of riches. But while enjoying the comforts of a moderate competency of property, with economy and careful management he was enabled to enjoy not only the luxury of counseling and aiding the poor in obtaining employment, but in some measure to relieve their immediate necessities. And he also had the pleasure of contributing to the support of public worship, and to the various benevolent societies for the promotion of Christianity. He was uniformly punctual in the payment of debts, and was never in the habit of employing others to do for him what he could as well do for himself; and he never was in the habit of procrastinating for tomorrow the work which might as well be done to-day. He was accustomed to have a place for everything, and to keep everything in its appropriate place.

# CHAPTER XII.

## PHYSICAL DISABILITY.

In consequence of being a close student for many years, in the latter part of life he suffered seriously from inflammation of the eyes, and hence he was prevented for several years from assuming any position of pastoral responsibility; and yet whenever any opportunity occurred for supplying vacant pulpits, or for preaching among the poor and destitute in scattered communities, he improved it—commonly with little or no pecuniary compensation.

# CHAPTER XIII.

### FIELDS OF HIS MINISTRY.

He employed his ministry chiefly in the vicinity of Providence, R. I., and Saratoga Springs, New York, where his family relatives resided. In each of these places he heartily co-operated in the organization of the Young Men's Christian Associations, and was accustomed to aid personally in sustaining their daily prayer meetings, and in promoting the revivals which blessed those places through their influence in the churches and in destitute fields. In several rural districts in the vicinity of these places, he expended much gratuitous missionary labor. And while encountering many hindrances in these very discouraging fields, by reason of the general apathy of the people on the subject of religion, he was in such cordial sympathy with all Christians of the different evangelical denominations, that he commonly enjoyed their confidence and co-operation, so that his preaching was frequently attended by the divine blessing in the awakening and conversion of many sinners among them.

At different periods he ministered, and acted as pastor for a few years, to large rural parishes (geographically considered), in the vicinity of both Providence and Saratoga, where he practically and successfully carried out his favorite theories of revivals, home evangelization, and the various moral reforms which he regarded as essentially connected with and as the fruits of true religion, as really as the branches are connected with the trunk and constitute a part of the tree. And finding his own peculiar theories and plans so uniformly blessed of heaven, in promoting genuine revivals of religion and home evangelization in the rural districts, he was greatly surprised to find it so difficult, if not almost impracticable to enlist the more conservative ministers and churches in the city and village where he resided at different periods, in special and successful efforts for moral reform and the salvation of men. In these prosperous, wealthy, and fashionable communities the competition and rivalry in building up large congregations were such, and the tendency to worldliness was so great in the churches, that the more popular, conservative and attractive ministers were commonly sought and employed, while the more spiritual, evangelical and effective were in less demand. Hence, revivals were less common and less powerful than in places where the temptations to worldliness and conservatism were not so great. As fascination and attractiveness in the ministry were in greater demand in such places than preaching, which is reproving and saving, the ministry seemed in some measure to be tempted to seek to please the people that they might be employed permanently, rather than to reform their characters and save their souls.

# CHAPTER XIV.

### FAITHFULNESS IN VIEW OF HINDRANCES.

With his strictly puritanical, religious opinions, and his belief that his Divine Master was the greatest and most perfect example of progressive and religious moral reformers, to be followed by his ministers, in opposing worldly conformity and popular sins, which weaken the spiritual power of the church, in promoting vital and practical godliness among the people at large, he found many and formidable obstacles to the effectiveness of his ministry. He thought that the power of the evangelical, revival and reformatory pulpit in the United States, in the denominations among which he chiefly labored, and after which he modeled his own ministry, culminated between the years 1820 and 1840, under the argumentative and pungent appeals of such ministers as Drs. Lyman Beecher, N. W. Taylor, Asahel Nettleton, N. S. S. Beman, E. N. Kirk and President Finney.

Hence he followed in a great degree their example. In common with many of the most successful ministers, he was not favored with a brilliant imagination, but relied mainly on the more solid and plain truths of the gospel for successful preaching. But he found that the increasing prosperity, luxury and worldliness of the period of his own ministry, from 1847 to 1870, had rendered such preaching much less acceptable to the churches and congregations in their back-slidden and thoughtless condition. Many had become, in the language of Scripture "high minded, lovers of pleasure more than lovers of God, having a form of godliness, but denying the power thereof." Under these circumstances, he found that too many professing Christians were unwilling to make such sacrifice of worldly indulgence and apathy as are involved in genuine revivals of spiritual religion, and therefore faithful and reproving preaching was unwelcome.

In order to be popular and acceptable, the minister must prophecy smooth things, and be peculiarly fascinating, pleasing and attractive, even though he sacrifice pungency and such practical application as stings the conscience, enforces responsibility and re-reforms the life.

Therefore, concerning such revival and reformatory preaching, many said: "This is a hard saying, who can hear it?" And for such as were unreasonably fastidious and capricious, his ministry had comparatively little fascination or magnetic attraction. And under such discouraging circumstances in efforts for the promotion of religion, he found consolation in the mysterious and righteous sovereignty and sufferance of Divine Providence.

"For promotion cometh neither from the east, nor from the west, nor from the south." "But God is the judge, He putteth down one and setteth up another."

A man's heart deviseth his way, but the Lord directeth his steps." Hence, we can learn that success or failure in connection with the best planned and intended efforts for promoting religion, as in all other departments of human endeavor, often transpire without visible or apparently adequate causes.

But under these circumstances of increasing discouragement and self-denial on the part of revival and reformatory ministers, the love of Christ and compassion for perishing sinners constrained him to be faithful to his Master and precious souls, to resist the popular current of laxity and worldliness, and to preach with much boldness, even at the sacrifice of much professional popularity against the prevailing usages and sins of the times. For, in reference to the strange and formidable hindrances frequently encountered in promoting spiritual religion, and in general reformatory work, he believed God appreciated and would reward good intentions and faithful efforts to promote his own glory. "And we know that all things work together for good to them that love God."

And we know that it is a great source of consolation to feel assured that "all things" including all our afflictions and hindrances in the work of the Lord, shall contribute to our ultimate welfare. "For our light affliction, which is but for a moment, worketh for us a far more exceeding and eternal weight of glory." Says a good commentator, "It is a privilege to suffer for the welfare of the Church." Paul regarded it as such, and rejoiced in the trials which came upon him in the cause of religion. The Saviour so regarded it and shrank not from the greatest sorrows involved in the work of saving his people." And the devoted and faithful minister, in preaching the gospel, should cheerfully "endure hardness as a good soldier of Jesus Christ."

For to do good, to defend the truth, to promote virtue, to save the souls of the perishing, is worth all that it costs; and he who accomplishes these things, by exchanging for them earthly comforts, has made a wise exchange. "The universe gains by it in happiness, and the benevolent heart should rejoice that there is such a gain, though attended with his individual and personal sufferings."

Ministers have a noble office. It is their privilege to make known to men the most glorious truths that can come before the human mind, and which are revealed by the gospel. Their business is not to strive, like the selfish devotees of the world, for mere gold, and honor, and worldly pleasures, but to show every man that he has a Saviour; that there is a hell to shun, and a heaven to obtain, and to " present every man perfect before God." With all its sacrifices and self-denials therefore, it is an inestimable privilege to be a minister of the gospel. For there is no man who diffuses through a community so much solid happiness; there is no man, the result of whose labors reaches so far into future ages. In such a work it is a privilege to exhaust our strength; in the performance of the duties of such an office, it is our honor to wear out life itself. Doing this, a man when he comes to die will feel that he has not lived in vain; whether his sphere of faithful service be limited by circumstances beyond his control, or whether he has been called in the order of providence to the widest and most extended spheres of influence. "For unto whomsoever much is given, of him shall much be required." "It is required of a steward that a man be found faithful." Such considerations as these encouraged this minister of Christ, whose life is here sketched, to faithfulness, amidst formidable obstacles and multiplied and repeated hindrances in preaching the glorious gospel of the blessed God to perishing sinners.

He was strongly impressed with the solemnity and force of Saint Paul's charge to Timothy in view of an approaching judgment: "Preach the word, be instant in season, reprove, rebuke, exhort, with all long-suffering and doctrine. But watch thou in all things, endure afflictions, do the work of an evangelist, make full proof of thy ministry." While this minister of Christ cherished an humble hope through grace of admission to heaven to enjoy the presence of every conceivable blessing, and the absence of every evil, and participation in the joys of "just men made perfect," who have been faithful in their efforts to turn men from sin to holiness, he experienced in the present life, something of the vagueness and hopelessness of all human aspirations.

Although by God's favoring providence, he thought

that his innocent and rational desires through life had been much more fully gratified than is common in the experience of the majority of mankind, yet from the midst of his ordinary cares, fears and griefs, he plainly saw that the day would never come in the present life in which cares, griefs and fears would not surround him, and therefore he desired "a better country, that is a heavenly," where such experiences should be ended. Though all the rest of the universe were given him to choose from, he realized that he could not find a place or condition where he could enjoy perpetual peace and rest.

He was convinced that if he could have all that this world could yield him, for the naming of it, so that every present desire should be gratified to the utmost, his weary soul would soon be found as far from rest as ever. For he knew that it was not in the power of the world to furnish men with perfect happiness, because "this is not our rest." "But there remaineth a rest for the people of God." Hence he hoped for special grace at the termination of this mortal life to exclaim with the inspired Psalmist, "Return unto thy rest, O my soul, for the Lord hath dealt bountifully with thee." And with the Apostle to say, "I am now ready to be offered, and the time of my departure is at hand. I have fought a good fight, I have finished my course, I have kept the faith. Henceforth there is laid up for me a crown of righteousness, which the Lord, the righteous Judge, shall give me at that day, and not to me only, but unto all them, also, that love his appearing."

# CHAPTER XV.

### REFLECTIONS AND ANTICIPATIONS.

Amid the strong temptations by which he was surrounded, he felt the need of constant and large measures of divine grace to preserve him in the narrow pathway of holiness, that he might be a minister of Jesus Christ, and that he might by patient continuance in well doing, seek for glory and honor and immortality and eternal life.

And in proportion as he manifested the spirit of his Divine Master amidst ordinary human infirmities, and was faithful in preaching the glorious gospel of the blessed God, let his ministerial brethren and Christian friends be stimulated by his example to greater earnestness in promoting the divine glory in saving souls. For God has said, " They that be wise shall shine as the brightness of the firmament, and they that turn many to righteousness as the stars forever and ever."

During his Chistian life, he aimed supremely to please his Heavenly Father. He aimed to glorify Christ who died to save him from sin and its dreadful penalty. He earnestly endeavored to follow His perfect example in all the experiences and pursuits of life. It was his controlling purpose to make the purifying and transforming religion of his Redeemer known as far as possible through his influence among mankind in Christian and heathen lands. He aimed to so live as to enjoy habitual cummunion with his Divine Redeemer, and derive his comfort and consolation from Him. And when such a man comes to die, has he not reason to rejoice in view of the controlling purposes of his past life, and in the hope of admission to his Saviour's more immediate personal presence in heaven, freed from sin and suffering? May we not, therefore, trust that for such a man to die is gain?

# CONCLUSION.

## REWARDS PROPORTIONED TO FAITHFULNESS.

While all Christians should be constrained by the love of Christ and compassion for the perishing, to labor diligently, to ameliorate the condition of the poor and the suffering, as well as to promote the holiness of their brethren and the conversion of sinners, yet like Moses, they may be encouraged to perseverance in doing good by " having respect unto the recompense of reward." They may be stimulated to increased zeal in every good work, by the consideration that personal holiness and active usefulness shall be the measure of the final reward of the saints in heaven. For it is written on the pages of inspiration, "they that be wise shall shine as the brightness of the firmament, and that they turn many to righteousness as the stars forever and ever."

We have the assurance that all who, in this life were humble followers of the Divine Redeemer, and by imitating him became eminently holy, and who went about doing good, "shall be admitted to heaven with his rapturous approval, "Well done, good and faithful servant, enter thou into the joy of thy Lord." "Then shall the righteous shine forth as the sun in the kingdom of their father."

But among the numerous and highly favored company who have been ransomed by the blood of the cross, and sing the song of Moses and the Lamb: "Unto Him that loved us and washed us from our sins in his own blood, to Him be glory and dominion forever and ever," "there are different degrees of glory and blessedness. There is one glory of the sun, and another glory of the moon, and another glory of the stars, for one star differeth from another star in glory. So also is the resurrection of the dead."

While all who have been justified by faith in Christ's atonement in life shall, in the life to come, be free from sin and suffering among "the spirits of just men made perfect," there will be different degrees of happiness in the heavenly world. Some in the lower types of piety, who have done but little in their Lord's vineyard are "saved so as by fire." Although they are delivered from all positive evil, they are only prepared for a low position, for comparatively a very moderate degree of enjoyment. While others of eminent holiness and greater capacities, and who have spent a life of greater devotion and of more active faithfulness in the service of their Divine Master, shall be elevated to higher and more rapturous felicity. "Wherefore, rather brethren give diligence to make your calling and election sure, so an entrance shall be ministered unto you abundantly into the everlasting kingdom of our Lord and Saviour Jesus Christ."

Some are barely saved, while others are welcome to higher seats in glory. And this diversity in glory and happiness among the saints hereafter will be both occasioned and measured by the difference in their holiness and usefulness in this life.

" He which soweth sparingly shall reap also sparingly, and he which soweth bountifully shall reap also bountifully." " Behold I come quickly and my reward is with me, to give every man according as his work shall be." " If we suffer, we shall also reign with him." " In Christ's parable of the pounds, which was evidently intended to convey to us some knowledge of our final judgment (observes a writer) we find that the reward bestowed by the nobleman upon his servants entrusted with the same deposit, was in every case exactly measured by the improvement that they made of it. The man who turned his trust to a two fold improvement, and he who gained with his pound five others, were rewarded successively by a ten and five-fold authority. And these facts in reference to heaven, as they are revealed for our encouragement and warning, so are they to this end frequently employed by the sacred penman. Therefore we need not hesitate to contemplate such motives, as a stimulus to Christian holiness and activity, because in some minds they might thus weaken their belief in that great cardinal truth of justification by faith alone. But the Apostles and early Christians had no such fear. They were covetous for a high place in heaven for all among whom they labored, and knowing that this was the reward of faithfulness here, they were constantly stimulating their hearers by such a prize to a life of holiness and usefulness." By this motive they pointed even their exhortations to pecuniary liberality, the very lowest and easiest form of beneficence. "Charge them that are rich in this world that they do good, that they be rich in good works, ready to distribute, willing to communicate, laying up in store for themselves a good foundation against the time to come, that they may lay hold on eternal life. A radical distinction, however, should in this connection be observed between the prize held out to the Christian, and all the glory and greatness of this world. In the present life the highest objects of ambition, and those which men most eagerly strive after, are such as by their nature can only be obtained by a few. That there should be any who are wealthy, powerful and celebrated, implies a necessity that there should be others who are poor, subject and obscure. That all, or even the greater part of any community should be rich men or rulers, or eminent, is not only impossible, but inconceivable. But this is not so of that prize which should excite the ambition of God's people." A few cannot win it to the exclusion of the rest. The elevation of one saint in heaven does not imply the depression of another. The power, and splendor, and riches of that better world may be enjoyed by an unlimited number, and by each in proportion to his fitness for it.

## CONCLUSION.

In the race for the most worldly objects, "they which run, run all, but one receiveth the prize," but in the pursuit of heavenly blessings, all may "so run as to obtain." Here then is the motive with which we would now urge Christian believers to a closer walk with God. No real progress in religion, no increase of personal holiness ever made in this world, will be unnoticed or unrewarded by God.

"Growing in grace here, and ever ascending in moral character nearer and nearer to God, we are thus continually adding new jewels to the crown of our everlasting rejoicing, and preparing for ourselves a high place of glory and blessedness in heaven."

> "In some fair and jeweled crown,
> That to the blest redeemed is given,
> Are stars that cast their brightness down,
> Loveliest among the gems of heaven."

It is the diadem he wears whose whole character on earth has been the most perfectly transformed into the image of Christ. "For so an entrance shall be ministered unto you abundantly, into the everlasting kingdom of our Lord and Saviour Jesus Christ." Thus (as a forcible writer has observed) "we are saved by grace (without personal merit on our part), and all the glory of salvation will belong to Christ. Yet our felicity in heaven is connected with our holiness and our works on earth. By eminent attainments in personal holiness and earnest and persevering efforts in advancing the cause of Christ, we are made to reflect his glory." Those who heard of the conversion of Saul, "glorified God in him."

All holy beings will glorify God in the redeemed from among men. As enjoying a peculiar felicity themselves, and as being instrumental in reflecting the glory of God, "they that turn many to righteousness shall shine as the stars forever and ever." They will have an eminence in glory, and bliss above the other inhabitants of heaven. No privilege did God ever commit to created intelligences, equal to that of laboring for the salvation of men. The reward of Christians for turning sinners to righteousness is somewhat in proportion to the value of the soul. A soul saved; what misery has it escaped! What joy awaits it in the interminable future! What can give Christians more joy than the recollection of labors, sacrifices, and prayers, by which others were saved? "There is joy in the presence of the angels of God over one sinner that repenteth." What joy then must the saint experience in spending an eternity in company with those who have been brought to heaven through his instrumentality. He will, in a sense, enjoy all the bliss that they enjoy, and all the glory that they reflect upon Christ; next to that which the redeemed will feel toward the triune God, will be the gratitude which they will feel toward those who are instrumental in turning them to righteousness.

O, how different the gains of those who labor for the treasures of earth, from the gains of those who labor to turn many to righteousness! There is no certainty of the continued enjoyment of earthly pleasures. All such enjoyment must be brief. "But they that turn many to righteousness, shall shine as the stars forever and ever." Not only bright, but everlasting joys, are in reserve for them. O, how glorious the prospect that beams upon their vision, when they finish their course and are about entering upon their reward! They are cheered in anticipation of the fulfillment of the gracious promises and final commendations of their Redeemer. "Be thou faithful unto death, and I will give thee a crown of life." "Well done, good and faithful servant, enter thou into the joy of thy Lord."

It has been well said that "we all desire glory." Men secure their highest glory by leading sinners to Christ. It was the ambition of Jesus to save men. For this He laid aside "the glory He had with the Father before the world was," that He might attain to this other glory. Men are invited to share a degree of this glory. His glory is absolute, while ours is relative. This is not salvation by works. Every citizen has the specific rights of citizenship, but superior service alone can secure him eminence. Men become citizens of the spiritual kingdom by faith, while special honor comes from noble service—which is great in degree as well as in nature. Wise working to overcome great difficulties, for an important end, brings great honor and enduring fame. To save the world requires all this, hence the glory of success. In this we do not deal with material substances. The painter and sculptor deal with passive matter, while soul savers have to deal with free spirits. Men with backs towards God, and faces towards hell, are to be aroused and turned about, against their inclinations and wills. Their closed ranks are to be broken, and they are to be saved one by one—torn out of their chosen relations and placed among people of another spirit.

For this work of faith, and labor of love, there is a glorious reward. "And they that be wise shall shine as the brightness of the firmament; and they that turn many to righteousness, as the stars forever and ever." That you may more highly appreciate this divine promise, go in the cloudless night, when the firmament of heaven is radiant with a thousand stars, gaze upward till your soul is overwhelmed with the inexpressible glory that surrounds you; then remember it is only the type of glory that awaits the faithful minister in the future world. But before he shall attain this blessedness, God will give him a foretaste of what is to come. The final approval of "Well done, good and faithful servant," may be reserved to the last day, when the seals and trophies of his ministry shall appear with him in glory; but even on earth, mingling with his sufferings and toil, communion with the Father, Son and Spirit, and the sweet consciousness of a successful instrumentality in the conversion of great multitudes of sinners, will constitute an amount of blessedness far transcending the enjoyment of men who live for this world, without God and the Christian hope.

Truly in keeping the commandments of God, there is great reward. We read that "one star differeth from another star in glory." Each star has its glory. But he who has turned many to righteousness, shall become a central star in a constellation of glorified spirits, saved by his instrumentality. Each shall reflect his proper light, but he shall shine with peculiar lustre and brilliancy, as the brightness of the firmament in the kingdom of God, "forever and ever, when sun, moon and stars wax old, and pass away from the firmament."

> "See in heaven the faithful preacher,
>   With the seals of his reward;
> How they throng to bless the teacher,
>   Who had led them to the Lord!
> Wise to save!—a sunlike lustre
>   Brightens all their home divine;
> As the stars—a radiant cluster—
>   They in endless glory shine!"

Behold the "unsearchable riches of Christ." As a writer has observed, "Not only does He forgive and save, but He notices with an approving eye everything that His people do for Him. He records their every word and act, put forth on His behalf, and even the most trivial service rendered to the obscurest of His followers. These He will recall, and crown with imperishable rewards at the last day. And, for your comfort, remember that the reward will be proportioned, not to your talents and opportunities, but to the use you make of them; not to what you accomplish, but to what you try to accomplish; not to the harvest you may reap here, but to the seed you may sow. 'Every man shall receive his own reward, according to his own labor.' Not according to his gifts, not according to his successes, not according to the worldly applause he may have won, but 'according to his labor.' Only be faithful

## CONCLUSION.

to your trust. Work from no sordid motive. Let the love of Christ constrain you to devote all your powers to His service, and when the labor of the day is over and you go up to the great harvest-home, you will be *satisfied*. 'Heaven and earth may pass away,' but 'you shall in no wise lose your reward.' You may be assured that every good act of your life, every kind word you may utter, every act of charity you may bestow however trifling, every tear you may prevent the shedding of, through sympathy with human suffering or otherwise, every pang of pain or sigh of distress you may alleviate, will increase your joy and blessedness in your heavenly home."

> You are daily making
> The robes that you will own,
> In the realms of light and beauty,
> And their splendor will be known
>
> By every deed of kindness,
> Your many acts of love,
> To earth's weary, stricken children,
> Reflected all above.
>
> When you raise a fallen brother
> Who has stumbled by the way,
> A robe of light is woven,
> Fraught with a heavenly ray.
>
> When you strive to banish error,
> To crush out weakness (sin)
> You are making golden sandals
> With which to enter in
>
> Those regions of the blessed,
> Which will in time be thine,
> And *charity* for *others*
> A veil will then entwine,

## CONCLUSION.

To shield perhaps the weaker.
   And as you then embrace,
This friend or stranger,
   A web of finest lace

Is yours for any purpose
   That you may need employ,
But the *prize* of prizes truly,
   Which gives the greatest joy,

Is the necklace on your bosom—
   Of pearls, a priceless gem,
And the crown upon your head,
   A wondrous diadem.

Whence comes it you will ask me,
   It is the tears you've shed
In lowly, sad contrition,
   When by the master led.

You have seen your sins as scarlet,
   With tears have washed them white,
Now, as reflected jewels,
   As radiant beams of light.

They are yours if you have *earned* them
   Each garment that you wear;
So weave in earnest,
   With thought and anxious care.

For *those* we cannot borrow,
   Nor beg, or steal or lend,
We clothe by our own effort,
   Pray God the grace to send

To clothe our spirits rightly
   With humility and love,
That we may be accepted
   Of God—who reigns above.

www.ingramcontent.com/pod-product-compliance
Lightning Source LLC
Chambersburg PA
CBHW032043230426
43672CB00009B/1446